ALASKA
ACCESSIBLE WILDERNESS
A TRAVELER'S GUIDE TO ALASKA'S STATE PARKS

BILL SHERWONIT

ALASKA NORTHWEST BOOKS™
ANCHORAGE ◆ SEATTLE ◆ PORTLAND

To my brother Dave and sister Karen. And to Ben Adelson, who helped me start along the writing path.

A portion of the royalties from sales of this book's first printing will be donated to the
Alaska State Parks Foundation, a nonprofit corporation whose purpose is to enhance the public's
enjoyment of Alaska's state parks while also helping to protect parks for future generations. Money raised
by the foundation is used for park projects that have the support of local park users as well as advisory boards
and park staff. Further information about the Alaska State Parks Foundation can be obtained
by writing to the foundation at P.O. Box 245001, Anchorage, AK 99524-5001.

Library of Congress Cataloging-in-Publication Data
Sherwonit, Bill.
    Alaska's accessible wilderness : a traveler's guide to Alaska's
state parks / by Bill Sherwonit.
        p. cm.
    Includes bibliographical references (p. 117) and index.
    ISBN 0-88240-471-7
    1. Alaska—Guidebooks. 2. Parks—Alaska—Guidebooks.
3. Wilderness areas—Alaska—Guidebooks. 4. Alaska—
Description and travel. 5. Parks—Alaska. 6. Wilderness
areas—Alaska. I. Title
F902.3.S38   1996
917.9804'5—dc10
                                                    95-52475
                                        CIP

ORIGINATING EDITOR: Marlene Blessing
MANAGING EDITOR: Ellen Harkins Wheat
EDITOR: Nicky Leach
DESIGNER: Elizabeth Watson
MAPS: Illustrations by Laszlo Kubinyi, type by Debbie Newell

PHOTOS: FRONT COVER: The Wood River Mountains reflected in Lake Kulik, Wood-Tikchik State Park. INSETS (LEFT TO RIGHT): Angler, Shuyak Island State Park; Dall sheep, Chugach State Park; Skier, Denali State Park. BACK COVER (TOP TO BOTTOM): Alaska brown bear; Nuka Island berries, Kachemak Bay State Park; Wild iris, Shuyak Island State Park; (right): Kayaker, Wood-Tikchik State Park. Page 1: The Wood River Mountains reflected in Lake Kulik, Wood-Tikchik State Park. 3: View from Peters Hills, looking north toward Alaska Range, Denali State Park. 4: Kayaker reflected in Lake Beverly, Wood-Tikchik State Park. 5: Sea otter. 6: Pond reflections, old-growth forest, Shuyak Island State Park. 7: Raindrops on skunk cabbage, Kachemak Bay State Park. 118: Angler fishing for silvers, Shuyak Island State Park. 120: Author Bill Sherwonit on Nuka Island, Kachemak Bay State Park.

PERMISSIONS: Portions of the Chilkat, Chugach, Kachemak Bay, Shuyak Island, and Wood-Tikchik chapters were previously published, in different form, in *The Anchorage Times, Anchorage Daily News,* and *ALASKA* magazine, and are reprinted here with permission.

Alaska Northwest Books™
An imprint of Graphic Arts Center Publishing Company
Editorial office: 2208 NW Market Street, Suite 300, Seattle, WA 98107
Catalog and order dept.: P.O. Box 10306, Portland, OR 97210
800-452-3032

Printed on acid-free recycled paper in the United States of America

FOREWORD

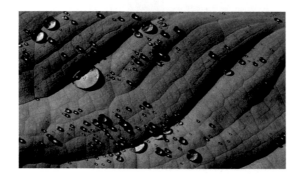

"State parks are a gift we give ourselves," a governor I once worked for told me.

After more than 20 years with Alaska State Parks, including nearly 13 years as director, I've watched our nation's youngest state park system blossom into America's largest state park system. I've been privileged to be part of the dreams and struggles of a special group of dedicated Alaskans who—despite seemingly insurmountable odds—gave to us all, and to those who will follow us, a magnificent gift: a system of 127 parks, recreation areas, and historic sites protecting 3.3 million acres of the best of the Great Land.

From the verdant rain forests of Southeast Alaska and the ocean fjords of Kachemak Bay to the glacier-carved peaks of the Chugach Mountains and the rolling birch forests of the Chena River, fully one-third of America's state park land is found in Alaska. And the parks' diversity and grandeur also offer abundant recreation opportunities: places to camp, fish, hike, ski. Alaska State Parks host 6 million visits each year.

These special places, the culmination of the vision and hard work of so many persons, should be viewed as nothing short of a "system of dreams"—the dreams of citizen activists who continue to dedicate themselves to the protection and wise stewardship of this outstanding park system.

As an active user of Alaska's parks, veteran outdoorsman and writer Bill Sherwonit's sensitive text and photographs are welcome. Bill knows Alaska's state parks as few others do, and is well qualified to present this first, comprehensive book on this vast park system.

Enjoy and protect them!

—*Neil C. Johannsen*
Former director, Alaska State Parks
November 29, 1995

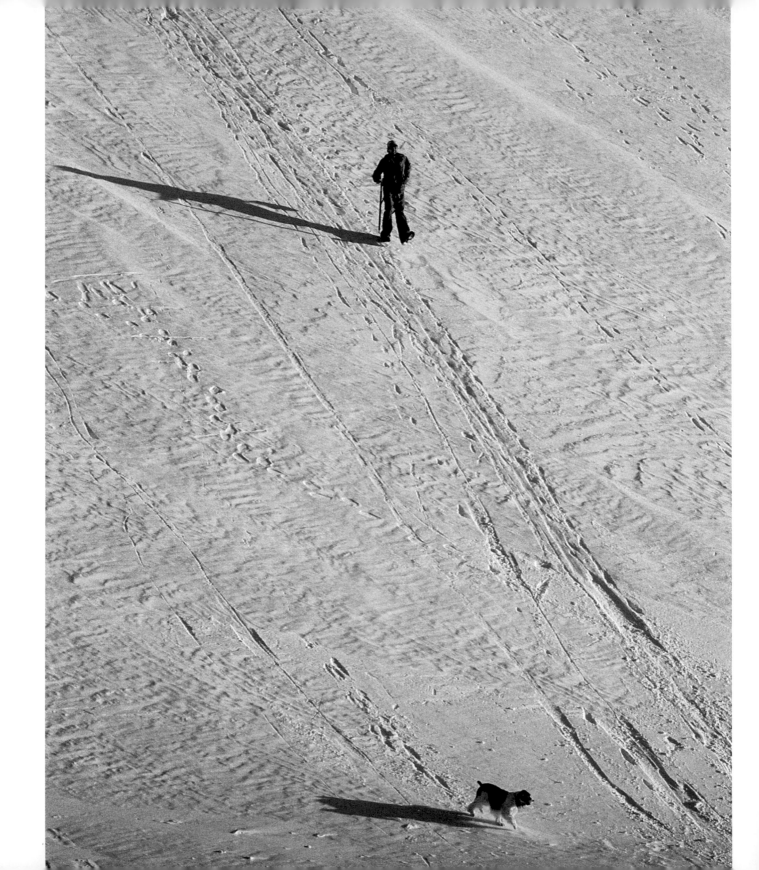

AN INTRODUCTION TO ALASKA'S ACCESSIBLE WILDERNESS

It's early April as I write this, and my mind keeps drifting toward the mountains east of Anchorage. From my desk, I can see some of the Chugach foothills—sweet inspiration. Two evenings ago, I drove up into the mountains at sunset—the nearest trailhead is less than 3 miles from my home—and visited Blueberry Hill, a low-rounded knob in Chugach State Park. I walked for a couple of hours, taking pictures and watching people ski, hike, glissade, and have fun in the mountains. Less than a mile away, still mostly covered in snow, was Flattop, probably the second most recognizable mountain in Alaska and certainly my favorite one to climb. This is where my relationship with Alaska's state parks took root in the early 1980s, shortly after I'd moved here from California to work at *The Anchorage Times*.

It began on a warm and sunny midsummer day when, along with dozens of other people, I hiked and scrambled up a narrow dirt trail that led to Flattop's summit and found wildness on the edge of town. It took me years, however, to fully appreciate the gift of Chugach State Park. This 495,000-acre "accessible wilderness" in Anchorage's backyard is a priceless sanctuary for Alaskans: a place to escape daily pressures and routines, to slow down and rediscover beauty, joy, and peace of mind—to reconnect with the wildness around us, and within.

My relationship with Chugach deepened in 1985, when I became *The Times*'s outdoors writer. This new niche gave me increased opportunities to explore the park, discover the breadth of its recreational appeal, learn its issues. But not until the 1990s did I begin to explore and appreciate several other state-owned jewels:

Wood-Tikchik, Kachemak Bay, Denali. All are part of a state park system that was born just 26 years ago.

In one glorious preservationist spasm, Alaska's lawmakers established four state parks, with more than 1 million acres among them, in the space of less than 5 months. That same year, 1970, state government created a Division of Parks and Outdoor Recreation to manage this new wealth of parkland. Nothing comparable has happened since, but there have been enough additions to make Alaska's state parks system the nation's largest and grandest. Alaska state parks now encompass 3.2 million acres, spread across nearly 130 separate units. Many of those units are roadside campgrounds, recreation areas, and historic sites, but also among them are several of our nation's premier wilderness parks.

Accessible wilderness is the theme that runs through this book—the thread that links the five state parks and one state wildlife preserve I've chosen to include: Kachemak Bay, Wood-Tikchik, Chugach, Shuyak Island, Denali, and Chilkat. Within their boundaries are some of Alaska's wildest and most pristine landscapes and ecosystems. In fact three of these state parks—Denali, Kachemak Bay, and Wood-Tikchik—include lands and waters that were once proposed for national park status. Instead, they were preempted by Alaska through rights given by the statehood act and later established as state parklands. They are places of glaciers and unscaled mountains, of centuries-old coastal rain forest and high alpine tundra, of salmon-rich streams, vast lakes, and remote islands, of grizzlies and wolves, eagles and swans.

◄ A hill-climber and his dog descend a snow-covered slope in April, Chugach State Park.

For all their wildness and unspoiled beauty, these six parklands are, by Alaskan standards, remarkably easy to reach and, in most cases, easy to explore. Geographically, they are spread through three of Alaska's six regions: Southeast, Southcentral, and Southwest. All but one—the Alaska Chilkat Bald Eagle Preserve—are within 325 miles of Anchorage, the state's primary visitor destination, as well as its largest city and the initial staging point for many wilderness journeys. And Chilkat is only a short plane ride from the state capital of Juneau, the largest city and top tourist destination in Alaska's Panhandle.

Four of the six parks are 10 miles or less from a highway or regional population center. Chugach and Denali state parks and the Chilkat Bald Eagle Preserve are connected to Alaska's road system, while Kachemak Bay is a short boat ride from Homer, an end-of-the-road tourist town 220 highway miles south of Anchorage. None of these four requires air service to reach the backcountry. While Wood-Tikchik's backcountry is most easily reached by plane, the park's lowermost lake is only 20 road miles from Dillingham, the largest city (population about 2,200) in the Bristol Bay region. The most remote of the state parks, Shuyak, is less than 100 air miles from Homer.

By contrast, wilderness within Alaska's national parks in many cases is remote, and therefore expensive to reach. Two-thirds of the units are more than 300 miles from Anchorage, and 5 of 15 are within the state's Arctic region. Backcountry trips in most of the national parks require the use of air-taxi services.

Most Alaska residents think the state parks tend to be more user-friendly than national parks, with campgrounds, public-use cabins, trail systems, and other facilities that make it easier to explore land- and seascapes without necessarily having to rough it. Shuyak, for example, has a system of public-use cabins, despite its remote location at the northern end of the Kodiak Archipelago. Both Denali and Chugach have road-accessible campgrounds, while those two plus Kachemak Bay and Shuyak Island have maintained trail systems that make backcountry travel easier. Even Wood-Tikchik, the largest and perhaps the most primitive of Alaska's state parks, has a campground and ranger cabin in its backcountry. Most of Alaska's national parks, on the other hand, have minimal public facilities, and some have none at all, an intentional decision by the National Park Service to minimize the human imprint on its lands.

The state has also emphasized the preservation of traditional uses by local residents, and there's less of what many Alaskans believe to be a "lock-up" mentality in the management of its parks. Finally, the wilderness areas of Alaska's state parks offer a broad spectrum of recreational uses: from hiking to sport hunting, skiing to snowmobiling, paddling to powerboating.

The parks that I've chosen to explore in this book are among the wildest and most alluring in Alaska's state parks system. Five of the six offer an inspiring mixture of wilderness, wildlife, scenic vistas, and outdoor recreation. The Alaska Chilkat Bald Eagle Preserve, the sixth, is famous for its wildlife—specifically bald eagles. The portraits I present in words and pictures are based on my journeys and the stories of people intimately connected to the locales. Visitor information is included for each of the six units, with tips on getting there, when to go, facilities and services, activities, suggested hikes, and all-important weather information.

There's also a chapter that summarizes Alaska's other state park units, which include recreation areas, marine parks, and historic sites. More general facts on Alaska's state parks system, and suggestions for backcountry travel, are scattered throughout the book. These include information on backcountry safety, camping, bear-human relations, user fees, air-taxi travel, and mosquitoes.

I invite you to join me on these adventures in Alaska's "other" parks. A well-kept secret among residents for years, Alaska's accessible state parks will delight you with their variety and richness and lure you into making your own discoveries.

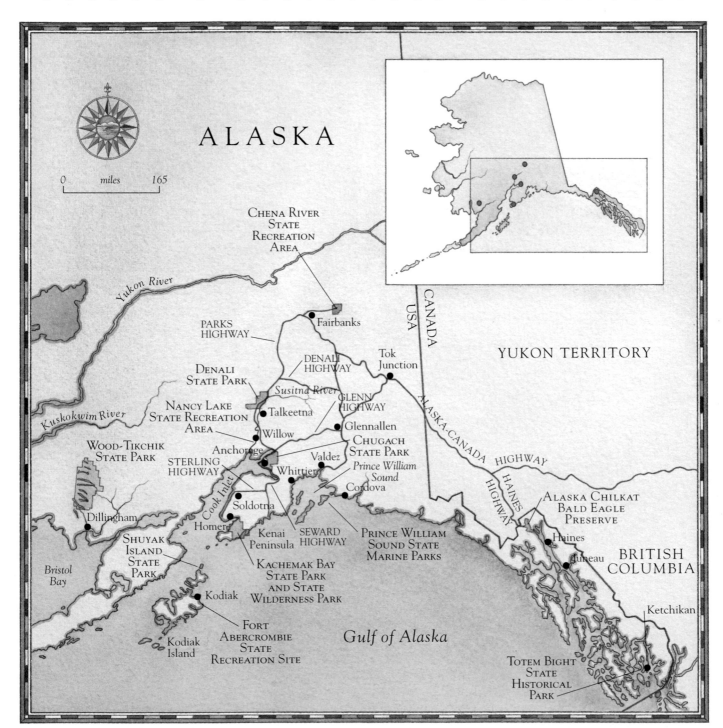

ALASKA

0   *miles*   165

CHENA RIVER
STATE
RECREATION
AREA

Yukon River

Fairbanks

PARKS
HIGHWAY

DENALI
HIGHWAY

Tok
Junction

YUKON TERRITORY

DENALI
STATE PARK

Susitna River

GLENN
HIGHWAY

USA

CANADA

Kuskokwim River

NANCY LAKE
STATE RECREATION
AREA

Talkeetna

Willow

Glennallen

CHUGACH
STATE PARK

WOOD-TICHIK
STATE PARK

Anchorage

Valdez

*Prince William
Sound*

ALASKA-CANADA

STERLING
HIGHWAY

Whittier

Cordova

HIGHWAY

HAINES

DILLINGHAM

Soldotna

Cook Inlet

ALASKA CHILKAT
BALD EAGLE
PRESERVE

HAINES

HIGHWAY

SHUYAK
ISLAND
STATE
PARK

Homer

Kenai
Peninsula

SEWARD
HIGHWAY

PRINCE WILLIAM
SOUND STATE
MARINE PARKS

Haines

Juneau

BRITISH
COLUMBIA

*Bristol
Bay*

Kodiak

KACHEMAK BAY
STATE PARK
AND STATE
WILDERNESS PARK

Ketchikan

Kodiak
Island

FORT
ABERCROMBIE
STATE
RECREATION SITE

Gulf of Alaska

TOTEM BIGHT
STATE
HISTORICAL
PARK

11

KACHEMAK 1

KACHEMAK BAY STATE PARK

WHERE LAND MEETS SEA

Having piled my gear safely above the outgoing tide, I shake José DeCreeft's hand and wish him a good flight back to Homer. "See you in eight days," I say to this veteran Alaska bush pilot, then add, "weather permitting." We both smile. In Alaska's backcountry, travel is always "weather permitting." With that in mind, I've brought enough food and fuel to last 2 weeks.

José and I push his yellow-and-green two-seater floatplane off the muddy bank, and my traveling companion of the past 25 minutes taxis a hundred yards before gunning the engine for takeoff. Within moments he's off the water and quickly gaining altitude. One circle, a wave, then silence.

I'm alone on Nuka Island, a 9-mile-long piece of land that's shaped—if you stretch your imagination—like a sea otter with too many legs. Nuka is reportedly derived from *nukaq*, a Yupik Eskimo name for young bull caribou. Since caribou have never occupied Nuka, I figure the island can just as easily remind me of an otter as it may have reminded someone else of a caribou.

On an August day like this, with the sun ablaze in a cloudless sky, Nuka is a short hop from the coastal town of Homer, a straight-line shot over Kachemak Bay, the Kenai Mountains, and Nuka Passage. But 2 to 3 miles off the Kenai Peninsula's outer coast, I'm worlds away from paved roads, fast-food restaurants, hot showers, computers, schedules, and people.

◀ A Klepper kayak sits on Kachemak Bay's Right Beach, a popular spot for ocean paddlers and other boaters.
▲ Blueberries collected on Nuka Island.

▲ Looking east, this view from Homer shows the Homer Spit, Kachemak Bay, and, across the bay, the western edge of Kachemak Bay State Park.

Once inhabited by a fox farmer and other home-steaders, Nuka was added to Kachemak Bay State Park in 1989. It no longer has any year-round or seasonal residents, and only rarely gets visitors (though that may change if plans for a wilderness lodge on private inholdings are realized). Except for a few abandoned buildings, and some scattered asphalt remnants left over from the *Exxon Valdez* oil spill, it's still pristine territory. The wildness is one reason I'm here. Another is solitude. In all my years of wilderness travel, I've never done an extended solo trip into the backcountry.

※

HOMER RESIDENTS HAVE officially proclaimed their community the "Halibut Capital of the World," but they could just as easily tout their town as the Gateway to Kachemak Bay State Park. Nearly all visits to Alaska's

oldest state park—it was established in June 1970, 2 months before Chugach State Park—begin and end there. Located on Kachemak Bay's northwestern shoreline, Homer started life as a turn-of-the-century coal company town (some linguists say Kachemak means "Smoky Bay," taken from an Aleut description of coal seams that once smoldered in bluffs above the bay). For the last few decades, though, commercial fishing and tourism have driven its economic engines, and more than 80,000 people now visit the area annually. Most come to sportfish for halibut and salmon; others relish the coastal scenery, wildlife, boating, and arts and crafts.

Officially, there are two state parks across the bay from Homer: Kachemak Bay State Park and Kachemak Bay State Wilderness Park. But for all intents and purposes, these two side-by-side parklands are treated as a

Cottonwood Creek

Chugachik Island

Glacier Spit

KACHEMAK BAY STATE PARK

KENAI NATIONAL WILDLIFE REFUGE

Kachemak Bay

Homer

Halibut Cove

Grewingk Lake

China Poot Bay

Halibut Cove Lagoon

GREWINGK GLACIER

Cook Inlet

Ranger Station

Leisure Lake

Wosnesenski

WOSNESENSKI GLACIER

River

Sadie Cove

KENAI FJORDS NATIONAL PARK

Tutka Bay

Herring Pete Cove

KENAI MOUNTAINS

Nuka Passage

Nuka Island

Northeast Cove

Tonsina Bay

Berger Bay

KACHEMAK BAY STATE WILDERNESS PARK

Westdahl Cove

KACHEMAK BAY STATE PARK

Port Dick

Gulf of Alaska

Gore Point

0   *miles*   6

▲ A floatplane ride provides spectacular views of the rugged and remote mountainous coast of Kachemak Bay State Park and Wilderness Park along Nuka Passage.

single entity. Together they encompass 380,000 acres of mountains, glaciers, lakes, river valleys, ice- and snowfields, coastal rain forest, alpine tundra, tidal marshes, sheltered bays, steep-walled fjords, waterfalls, storm-wracked outer coast, and ocean. No other Alaska state park, and only a couple of national parks, can boast such a variety of habitats, wildlife, and recreation. The region's richness is further reflected by the presence of two adjacent conservation units to the northeast: the Kenai National Wildlife Refuge and Kenai Fjords National Park. Yet for all of that, Kachemak Bay remains one of Alaska's lesser-known parks. Visitors to Homer may marvel at the mountains, glaciers, and forested coastline across the bay, but only one in four

will set foot in the park, less than 10 miles away. The reason is simple: there are no roads from Homer to the park; the only access is by boat or floatplane.

Eighty percent of those who do cross over to the park stay within a narrow strip of coastline from the Glacier Spit south to Halibut Cove, China Poot Bay, and Leisure Lake—an area with good fishing, kayaking, and (in summer) daily water-taxi service. It's also where the park's visitor facilities—public-use cabins, trails, campgrounds, and ranger station—are concentrated. And on private land, within or adjacent to the park, are a wilderness lodge, bed-and-breakfasts, even a restaurant and art shops. Beyond this slice of coast, the park remains primitive and largely unpeopled.

HERE ON NUKA, I take a few minutes to reconnoiter my new neighborhood, a quiet forest-sheltered lagoon at the end of Berger Bay. Walking toward a small unnamed creek that empties into the lagoon, I spook a flock of gulls, which take flight with loud protesting screeches. Less than 10 feet wide, and only inches deep on average, the creek seems an unlikely spawning stream, yet it manages to support a small run of pink salmon. A dozen pinks circle in the salt water, but it's one that lies atop a boulder, headless, that catches my attention, just as it did the gulls'. To them, it is a meal; to me, it's bear sign. I quickly scan the forest, creek bed, lagoon; seeing nothing that resembles a black bear, I take a deep breath and back away. Time to end my reconnaissance and look for a tent site.

My plan is to set up a base camp from which I'll explore Nuka Island and its coast. An hour of searching fails to reveal any place nearby that's reasonably flat and dry, well drained, above the high-tide line, and within easy walking distance of a creek, yet away from either bear sign or berry patches. Finally settling on a site that's within 50 feet of the lagoon's mud bottom, I pitch my tent at the fringes of a grassy meadow, in the company of alders and wildflowers. Here, where meadow meets forest, I'll be able to keep close tabs on my Klepper (a collapsible kayak easily packed in a plane). And there's a knoll above me, with trees perfectly spaced for a tarp, that will serve as my cooking/eating station; it's far enough from my tent that cooking smells shouldn't be a problem. Because I'm in bear country, the food I've brought is minimally odoriferous, but bears have a superior sense of smell and even freeze-dried foods could lure one in.

It's a good spot, the best I've found along the lagoon, but still I'm uneasy. I've seen bear scat and trampled grass within 100 feet of camp, and bushes laden with ripe blueberries and salmonberries line Nuka's shoreline. My first night on the island, finding it hard to settle down, I lie in the sleeping bag and listen to night sounds. There's splashing in the lagoon. Probably only salmon jumping, I tell myself. Alone, surrounded by darkness, old anxieties rise in a way they haven't for years. As usual I've brought no gun, only pepper spray. Bear "repellent" we Alaskans call it, half in jest. Intended as a last (and perhaps desperate) line of defense against bears, the spray offers some peace of mind, but I hope I never have reason to test its effectiveness. I listen for splashes and footsteps a while longer, then put in earplugs to cut off the night sounds and fall into a restless sleep.

By the third day of my island visit I'm feeling more at home. I now have a niche defined by my campsite, kayak, and cooking area. But it's only a temporary one; I'll leave a minimal imprint on my passage here. While any traces of my brief stay will soon be gone, it's taken several years of winter storms to erase most evidence of the 1989 EXXON *Valdez* oil spill.

"It was on Nuka that the reality of the spill hit me; I saw the horrible things it was doing," says Jeff Johnson, the park's first ranger, who now works out of state parks headquarters in Anchorage after 10 years at Kachemak Bay. "Birds so covered with oil you could hardly recognize them were desperately preening themselves. I know it sounds strange, but they would look at you almost like they'd been betrayed."

Oil reached Nuka Island's shores in early April, 12 days after the tanker ran aground on Bly Reef and spilled 11 million gallons of North Slope crude into Prince William Sound. Hardest hit was Northeast Cove. Surrounded by steep rock walls that form a natural amphitheater, the cone-shaped bay became Nuka's "only major [oil] collection area," Johnson recalls, but oil also blackened beaches at Berger and Mike's Bays and Southwest Cove.

By the end of April, nearly the entire outer coastline of Kachemak Bay State Park and State Wilderness Park had been polluted by the spill, more than 100 miles in all. (Other traces of the spill—oil sheens, tar balls, and mousse, a thick, chocolaty emulsion of oil and water—eventually drifted into Kachemak Bay itself.)

17

▲ Tent camping on Nuka Island: a campsite established on the fringes of a coastal meadow provides easy access to the nearby saltwater lagoon and Berger Bay.

"We didn't get near the [media] attention that Prince William Sound did, but some of our areas were hit just as bad. We had the most significant oiling outside the Sound," says Johnson, who spent the entire summer monitoring spill damage and cleanup efforts. "You can't imagine what it was like. In places we were knee-deep in mousse. There were piles and piles of dead seabirds and otters. We tried to retrieve as many as possible, to keep them out of the food chain; sometimes you couldn't identify what you were pulling out of the mire."

In July, a group of Homer residents exasperated by official spill cleanup efforts created the Homer Area Recovery Coalition. With money raised through grants and private donations, HARC set up camp at Mars Cove in Kachemak Bay Wilderness State Park and began its own cleanup. While EXXON's crews used high-pressure hoses, vacuum equipment, and fertilizers on shoreline cleanups, HARC's citizen volunteers—from places as distant as Hawaii and Switzerland—relied on manual labor and rock-washing machines created by Homer's Bill Day. Controversial in some quarters, HARC's cleanup earned the park's unofficial blessing. "This is the people's park," says district ranger Roger MacCampbell. "If people want to clean it, so be it. We saw it as part of the healing process."

Five years later, most of the oil is gone, cleaned by crews or coastal storms. But, says Johnson, "if you know where to look, you can still find asphalt out there. In

18

BACKCOUNTRY SAFETY

Before setting out on a backcountry trip, contact the rangers at the park you'll be visiting for further information about the area, travel tips, and any hazards. Leave your itinerary with someone you trust, including your planned route, expected date of return, and emergency phone numbers.

Expect Alaska weather to be changeable and pack accordingly. Summer daytime temperatures range between the 40s and 80s, while nighttime temperatures may dip below freezing. Winter-like storms are possible at any time of year, particularly in the mountains. Bring adequate clothing (discussed below) to avoid hypothermia—a cooling of the body's core temperature—should conditions turn wet, cold, and windy. While traveling, drink plenty of fluids, eat well, and pace yourself, so you don't become exhausted. If a member of your party becomes hypothermic (signs include shivering, slurred speech, and clumsiness), take steps immediately to remedy the situation: set up a shelter, have the person change into warm and dry clothing, administer warm nonalcoholic liquids, and perhaps build a fire. In extreme cases place the victim, unclothed, in a sleeping bag with one or two other naked people, to transfer body heat.

Always pack the essentials: compass, map, extra clothing, food, water, flashlight, waterproof matches, fire starter, first-aid kit, and pocket knife. Other Alaskan essentials include high-quality rain gear, insect repellent, sunglasses, and sunscreen.

Bring clothing made of wool or synthetics such as polypropylene, Capilene®, or fleece, which offer insulation even when wet. Layers work best, as they can be added or removed as the weather changes. Other essentials include durable wind and rain shells, a wool or synthetic hat, gloves or mittens, sturdy hiking boots, and, in coastal areas, rubber boots.

Anticipate weather delays, especially when traveling to and from wilderness areas by air taxi or boat. Bring extra food and fuel, and don't travel in marginal weather: it's not worth the risk. Ocean paddlers should take a local tide book and pay attention to tidal fluctuations.

Many of Alaska's rivers and lakes contain *Giardia*, a microorganism carried in the feces of many mammals that can cause an intestinal disorder. Boil water vigorously for at least 1 minute or use a water filter.

Good route-finding and map-reading skills are vital when traveling through Alaska's wilderness. Learn and practice proper safety and emergency techniques before heading into challenging wild country. Excellent resources are Don Graydon's *Mountaineering: The Freedom of the Hills,* which includes chapters for all wilderness travelers, and Helen Nienhueser and John Wolfe's *55 Ways to the Wilderness in Southcentral Alaska.* Wilderness skills classes and training are available in Anchorage through the University of Alaska Anchorage's Alaska Wilderness Studies Program, (907) 786-4066; Alaska Pacific University's Outdoors Program, (907) 564-8308; Recreational Equipment Inc., (907) 272-4565; and Alaska Mountaineering & Hiking, (907) 272-1811.

July, if the weather's been warm enough, there'll be puddles of oil." I haven't seen any signs in my short stay.

Beyond the harm it did to coastal habitat and wildlife, the 1989 spill had an unexpected secondary impact on Kachemak Bay's state parks. "More people visited the outer coast than in the last 200 years combined," MacCampbell explains. "People who never would have gone there became exposed to the abundant wildlife, the kayaking potential. It piqued people's interest." In one year, the number of businesses requesting permits to operate in the wilderness park jumped from 0 to 12, most of them outfitters and guides. Yet even with the increased interest, there remain places you can go days, or even weeks, without seeing another person. Nuka is one. In 8 days, I'll hear a handful of planes and see a couple of boats in Nuka Passage, but I won't meet another person until José returns.

I share the lagoon and forest fringes with a variety of wildlife, mostly birds. Among my most active, or at least highest-profile, neighbors are four belted kingfishers. They're very handsome birds, with a feathery crest atop their head and a white "collar" that contrasts sharply with their predominantly blue-gray head, back, and wings. Persistent, loud talkers, kingfishers' conversations are a blend of high-pitched screeches and raspy, rattling chatter. They're also wonderfully playful creatures, often chasing each other around the lagoon. Darting. Diving. Swooping. And, it turns out, they're also the cause of much of the splashing I hear. One morning I watch a kingfisher catch several minnow-sized fish. From its dead spruce perch, the bird swoops down, hovers momentarily, then plunges headfirst into the lagoon. An instant later it emerges with a fish and returns to its perch. There the fish is swallowed whole, head first. Another neighbor is a harbor seal that makes daily forays into the lagoon, hunting for salmon. It too is a splasher. Seeing and hearing these animals has helped me sleep easier at night. Nighttime splashes no longer keep me awake.

Here, at the end of the lagoon, I'm enclosed by forested hills that rise to 1,500 feet (Nuka's high point is 2,107 feet). The hills protect me from coastal gales but also limit my views. To see the larger world of Nuka Island, I go for daily paddles into Berger Bay and occasionally beyond. But not too far beyond. Alone, with limited ocean-kayaking experience, I choose caution over ambition. I'm content to hug Nuka's convoluted western shore, where a series of five squiggly shaped bays offers shelter from prevailing ocean winds. Only 9 miles separate the island's northern and southern tips, but there's two to three times that much shoreline on Nuka's inner side. My reach extends no farther north than Herring Pete Cove, about 5 miles from camp by kayak. The scale of things is humbling. I'm a gnat on the island's skin; in 8 days I'll explore perhaps 10 percent of Nuka's coastline and barely penetrate its wooded, untrailed interior. And Nuka, on most maps of Alaska, is an unnamed ink spot on the edges of the Gulf of Alaska's blue vastness. I shrink further, to microorganism size, a dot within a dot.

A southerly appendage, my lagoon is connected to Berger Bay's open waters by a channel that's less than a football field long and 10 yards wide. About a mile across at its mouth, the funnel-shaped bay has a community of islets within its borders; most are wooded, but a couple on the fringes are bare rock and are used as rookeries by cormorants and gulls. I tour the bay daily, always finding something new. One day it's a female sea otter with pup. On others it's a black bear (about a mile from camp), the remnants of a fox-farming station, an army of jellyfish, a loon, a pod of porpoises.

One of my greatest pleasures is to sit in my kayak, at twilight, in the middle of Berger Bay. Now shadowy and still, its only sounds are songbird whistles, the occasional splash of jumping salmon, and the tinkling of water droplets as they fall from my paddle into the bay. Settled into serenity, I look eastward past the islets to Nuka Passage (used by migrating humpback and gray whales) and the Kenai Peninsula. Only 3 miles away, the mainland seems a distant, tumultuous otherworld. Through binoculars, I watch huge waves crash against rocky cliffs and sandy beaches. Their relentless pounding comes to me as a deep muted rumble, an endless throbbing. Beyond the beaches, poking below dark clouds, is the pale blue tongue of an anonymous glacier that feeds an unnamed river. It flows out of the Kenai Mountains, among peaks also without names and likely unclimbed. Rising 2,000 to 3,000 feet above Nuka Passage, the mountains are lush, dark green. With more-powerful binoculars or a spotting scope, I might see mountain goats. All this, too, is within Kachemak Bay State Park.

These evening meditations sometimes take me over the mountains and back to the bay for which this park is named. Though I've lived in Alaska since 1982 and visited Homer many times, Kachemak Bay is still largely a mystery to me. This summer is the first that I've spent more than a day or two on its eastern shores. Now I've camped at Right Beach (a favorite with kayakers and other boaters), walked among rainbow-colored fields of wildflowers on the Alpine Ridge Trail, harvested mussels in China Poot Bay, and watched a coyote prowl the shore of Neptune Bay. And I've begun to learn fragments of this 39-mile-long, cornucopia-shaped estuary's natural and cultural history.

Kachemak is biologically rich enough to be labeled an "aquatic nursery" by biologists and designated a critical habitat area by the state. Salmon, halibut, shrimp, herring, crabs, clams, harbor seals, sea otters, porpoises, and occasionally sea lions and whales inhabit its waters. Gull Island, a tiny basalt outcropping 3 miles from the Homer Spit (and outside the park), is one of the region's largest bird rookeries, a breeding ground for gulls, kittiwakes, cormorants, murres, puffins, and guillemots. Each spring and fall, tens of thousands of shorebirds, seabirds, and waterfowl stop in Kachemak Bay on north- and southbound migrations, to feed in tidal pools and mudflats.

Attracted by the bay's abundance, seafaring Natives known to anthropologists as the Ocean People settled here nearly 5,000 years ago. They were followed, from 1800 B.C. to A.D. 500, by at least four other prehistoric cultures, which left behind stone tools, pictographs, house pits, and middens (piles of discarded bones and shells). Centuries later came the white explorers, prospectors and miners, trappers, hunters, fishermen, and homesteaders. "The fact that people have lived here for thousands of years tells you something about the richness, the power, of this place," says Mike McBride, the owner of a wilderness lodge and a Kachemak Bay resident since 1969. "The spirit of the ancient peoples is still here, if you allow yourself a little flight of imagination."

My fourth day at Nuka I leave the protected confines of Berger Bay and travel north to Herring Pete Cove, named after "Herring" Pete Sather, who lived here from the 1920s to the 1960s with his wife, Josephine, and operated the island's fox farm. After 2 days of mostly clouds and drizzle, the sun has returned and temperatures soar toward 70° Fahrenheit.

Turning into the cove, I see a group of sea otters several hundred feet off my bow. One of the them—a sentry perhaps?—approaches at an unhurried pace to within 50 feet of the kayak. It rolls, backpaddles, and "stands up" for a better look. Then, either disinterested or leery, it dives and swims off, resurfacing among its companions. Fifteen minutes later, now well within the cove, I'm approaching a kelp bed when another form takes shape within the seaweed. First I notice what seems to be a webbed foot. Next a head. Then two heads. It's an adult female otter, lying on her back and holding a pup. Both, apparently, are napping, and the gentle splash of waves on a nearby islet is enough to camouflage my paddle strokes. Almost on top of them, I try to stop the kayak, but the loud splash of my back-paddling alerts the otters, who abruptly sit up and turn my way. The female, pup in her grasp, stares a second or two, as if in disbelief; she must be quite flabbergasted by the sudden appearance of this strange creature. Then, keeping me in sight, she backpaddles away and dives.

Topographic maps of the area show four cabins along the shores of Herring Pete Cove, but from the water I can see only one: a large, rusted, corrugated metal structure. No one has lived here since the early

▲ A tidal pool in Kachemak Bay ▶ Late evening alpenglow on the Kenai Mountains
is reflected in Hazelle Lake, within Kachemak Bay State Park.

1980s, and I'd like to think the cove will remain unin-
habited, that its buildings will eventually be absorbed
by the island. But the University of Alaska, which
owns 46½ acres of land on Nuka Island, intends otherwise. University officials want to lease their land to
someone who'll build and operate a commercial lodge
facility at either Herring Pete Cove or Mike's Bay just
to the south. Unknown to me, they are issuing Requests
for Proposals even as I visit Nuka. The wilderness lodge
they envision would offer whale watching, sea kayaking,
fishing, and wildlife photography opportunities. Exactly
how large it would be, and the number of people it
might accommodate, are unknown as I write this.

Those plans worry me. Meadows, marshes, muskegs,
and backwater lagoons on Nuka Island's western shoreline cannot sustain heavy traffic. With one or more
lodges operating throughout the summer season, the
flow of human traffic will likely cause significant
damage to plants, soils, and perhaps wildlife. The state
also plans to build two recreational cabins on Nuka
Island. At best, they'll be a mixed blessing; cabins may
help to alleviate camping impacts, but their presence
will inevitably attract more human traffic to the island.

22

Not that the Division of State Parks has much choice in the matter: legislation that added Nuka Island to Kachemak Bay State Park required "one or two public-use cabins." It can be argued, of course, that I have no reason to fuss; I too am drawing attention to Nuka, by writing about the island. And now that I've had the pleasure of enjoying Nuka's wildness, why should I wish to restrict others? As usual, in wilderness matters, there are no easy answers. But one thing seems clear: Nuka is a place that deserves minimal development, without crowds or tours.

Though I spend most of my time around the lagoon or on the water, I take a few short walks into Nuka's coastal rain forest. Not to get anywhere, but simply to be with it. One afternoon, I climb above camp and find a seat among the trees, using a hemlock as a back rest and thick moss as a seat cushion. Nuka supports a mixed Sitka spruce–hemlock forest, yet nearly all the trees around me are hemlocks. It makes sense; they need a lot of moisture to thrive, and this lower hillside is exceedingly moist. Elsewhere, especially at higher elevations, spruce dominates.

Propped against the hemlock, I absorb the forest's touch—the velvety softness of moss and the hard, scratchy unevenness of tree bark. A tart berry taste lingers on my tongue, and a faint evergreen scent pricks at my nose. Bands of sunlight filter brightly through the trees—such a difference from the darkly mysterious and foreboding forest of night. Large flocks of songbirds rustle in the canopy, while hidden robins and varied thrushes call cheerfully. One thing I miss is the amiable chatter of squirrels. Their absence surprises me at first, but shouldn't. To reach the island, any mammal would have to swim 3 miles across Nuka Passage, or be introduced by humans.

I try to guess the forest's age. The largest trees on this hill are 1 to 1½ feet in diameter, but on other slopes I find hemlock and spruce up to 3 or 4 feet wide. Some of these trees are probably 300 to 400 years old. The forest's understory is low to the ground and consists mostly of berry plants, moss, and young hemlocks;

walking is easy. Along streams and the margins of some clearings, the forest is more of a jungle. Berry plants, devil's club, ferns, and alders huddle in dense thickets.

I think back to a time earlier this summer when, on a visit to China Poot Bay—about 4 miles across Kachemak Bay from the Homer Spit—I'd spent time with another tree, an ancient Sitka spruce, 4 feet wide near its base. To Mike and Diane McBride, who live at China Poot Bay and run Kachemak Bay Wilderness Lodge, the spruce is sacred—a symbol of the area's precious coastal rain forest. To loggers, this same spruce symbolizes money; not so many years ago, they had marked it for timber harvest. And so the tree takes on a meaning beyond its arboreal splendor: it is a symbol of conflicting values and an 18-year saga involving thousands of acres of old-growth rain forest within Kachemak Bay State Park.

If you dig deep enough, you find that the roots of this conflict reach far into Alaska's past. But for simplicity's sake, we'll begin in 1971, with congressional passage of the Alaska Native Claims Settlement Act. ANCSA was the government's way of compensating Native Alaskans for the loss of lands they'd historically occupied. It awarded them $90 million and 40 million acres of land, to be divided among 13 regional corporations and dozens of village associations. In 1975, the Seldovia Native Association—a village group based in Seldovia, about 7 miles west of the park—selected its 69,000 acres of land. Among its choices were 29,400 acres in the heart of Kachemak Bay State Park, directly across from Homer. Two years later, SNA and the Alaska Department of Natural Resources began negotiating a land swap. Discussions continued off and on for nearly a decade, with only two minor land trades. Frustrated with the lack of progress, SNA chose another route: in 1987, it sold logging rights on 12,000 acres of its park inholdings to the Timber Trading Company. The ensuing public outcry spurred state officials into reopening negotiations with SNA the following year. Some months later, a group of Homer residents formed the Kachemak Bay Citizens

Coalition to lobby for a buyback of SNA's inholdings. "These Native-owned lands are where we and the tourists go," wrote Homer activist Janice Schofield. "[The buyback area] is where we hike, camp, fish, and get revitalized. The quality of all our lives is interconnected with this land. . . . Imagine Kachemak Bay State Park with a gigantic gouge in its center."

State negotiators finally struck a deal with SNA and Timber Trading in 1990: $20 million for 24,000 acres of inholdings. But the House of Representatives rejected that plan on a 20 to 20 vote. Buyback bills were reintroduced to the state legislature in 1991 and 1992, but again each fell victim to politics. Despite the setbacks, public interest broadened. Buyback supporters came to include not only environmental activists but also sport and commercial fishermen, local businesses, educators, recreational groups, the Homer City Council, Kenai Peninsula Borough, the Alaska Visitors Association, and a former governor, Jay Hammond. More than 8,000 people, from communities throughout Alaska, signed buyback petitions.

"It was the biggest grassroots campaign anybody had ever seen," marvels local resident Anne Wieland, "a broad-based, nonpartisan coalition of people who love Kachemak Bay for many different reasons." A retired Anchorage teacher who now lives in Homer, Wieland first visited the park in 1975, the same year that SNA made its land selection. Later she bought land "right on its doorstep." As one of the buyback's principal lobbyists from 1991 to 1993, she found the park a source of inspiration: "I'd talk to the trees, seek their guidance. I would ask them what to do next—just a simple answer. I'd say, 'Help us to help you.' "

The long-running struggle to preserve Kachemak Bay's forest, and to make the park whole again, finally ended in 1993, when $22 million from *Exxon Valdez* oil-spill settlement funds were used to buy back SNA's remaining 24,000 acres and all timber and mineral rights on those lands. "Alaskans made it clear that this is a special place—a place of unimaginable potential for recreation, refreshment, education, and inspiration,"

▲ Diane McBride stands beside an ancient Kachemak Bay Sitka spruce tree.

says Mike McBride, whose lodge is the same age as the neighboring park. "And we don't want anyone messing around with it."

Standing with her husband beside the ancient spruce, Diane McBride looks upward and smiles. "It's like a dark cloud has lifted," she says. "The uncertainty was worst—but now it's over. We kept the park whole."

—∽∾—

OUT OF THE FOREST, and back to the ocean. Just south of Berger Bay is Westdahl Cove, but to get there I must paddle around a narrow, rocky peninsula that juts into

25

Nuka Passage. There's nothing here to block the wind, and the closer I get the bigger the waves become. On two different occasions I'm turned back by high winds and big rollers that crash with a roar against the cliffs.

I decide to give it one final try my last evening at Nuka. Both wind and waves have diminished, though there's still a steady breeze and 4- to 5-foot swells. Keeping a safe distance from the cliffs, I paddle around the corner into milder water, where I'm immediately met by a squadron of horned puffins; they circle me, wings beating furiously, then spiral away. Westdahl's 30- to 40-foot-high rock walls are ideal nesting grounds for these small black-and-white seabirds, which get their name from the fleshy black projections above each eye. With penguin-like coats, large red-tipped yellow beaks, and a Chaplinesque waddle, puffins are among the most distinctive of Alaska's seabirds, and a favorite of bird-watchers. To meet them here is an unexpected delight.

I linger just a few minutes in puffin domain, then return to the point, where a couple of monster rollers rise up to engulf me. I catch a ride on the second one and peer into a trough that looks 8 to 10 feet deep, maybe deeper. Then the wave rolls on, trailing me in its wake. My heart is racing, but these rollers aren't breaking until they reach shore. By angling across the swells, I'm carried back into calmer water. I try to imagine crossing Nuka Passage; it's a frightening thought.

Toward the end of my Nuka stay I begin to slow down, to experience some indefinable shift in consciousness. I look less often at my watch and pay more attention to the cycle of tides emptying and refilling the lagoon twice daily. Happily propped against a tree, I read for hours on end or simply sit, letting the forest energy wash over me. I walk barefoot in moss, then go down to the lagoon and let mud squish between my toes. And I hear sounds. Creek songs maybe, or forest voices. There is music here, behind the rush of wind and water, the rustle of grass and needles.

Roughly circular in shape and 300 feet across, with a mixed mud-and-gravel bottom, the lagoon is inhabited by all manner of intertidal creatures. I watch as hermit crabs come out of hiding with the incoming tide and scurry about in their sideways fashion, scavenging for food and chasing one another. Do they have territories? Or do they seek new shelters? Or mates? Whatever their reasons, they wage ferocious battles with each other. With soft bodies protected by the armor of their borrowed shells, they extend pincers and wave them about like swords. Parrying, thrusting, they remind me of dueling knights. I wonder if their world is as silent as it seems, or if they're speaking in voices I can't hear. Months later I get at least a partial answer to my questions; in A *Natural History of the Senses*, Diane Ackerman writes, "The ocean looks mute, but is alive with sounds . . . locked within the atmosphere of water." But what sounds, if any, do the hermits make?

There must be tens of thousands of hermit crabs in this one lagoon, but snails are even more prolific; millions cover the mud and rock flats at low tide. In places it's impossible to avoid walking on them; every step produces faint crunching sounds. Barnacles and mussels are two other abundant residents, but less visible are sculpins, eels, red-shelled crabs, and tiny sea anemones. Saltwater grasses and several varieties of seaweed poke out of the lagoon at low tide, giving it a green-and-yellow hue that smells strongly of salt, mud, and organic decay. High tide adds salmon, jellyfish, schools of minnow-sized fish, and occasionally a seal or sea otters to the mix. And there are the birds, of course: the frolicking, diving kingfisher family; squawking black-and-blue Steller jays that come to inspect my camp; bald eagles roosting in shoreline trees and rising high above the island on late-afternoon thermals; garrulous gulls; and an orchestra of songbirds.

It ends too soon, this island reverie. Just before 3 P.M. on my last day on Nuka, a faint droning noise reaches me and grows steadily louder. Suddenly José DeCreeft's yellow-and-green floatplane swings around a corner into view, circles once, twice, then lands smoothly on the bay. José is right on schedule, the first person I've seen in 8 days. I'm happy to see him—ready, once again, for human company.

▲ **Steller jay, at sunrise**

IF YOU GO

Getting There: Located at the southern tip of the Kenai Peninsula in Southcentral Alaska, Kachemak Bay State Park and Wilderness Park are accessible by boat or floatplane. The primary gateway community is Homer, 220 road miles south of Anchorage and less than 10 miles from the park's western border. Once in the park, the primary means of transportation is boat or foot.

Weather: Normally cool, wet, and often windy; severe coastal storms may occur with little warning. Along the Gulf of Alaska coast, winds greater than 40 mph and seas of 15 feet or more are not uncommon. Summer daytime temperatures throughout the park range from the 40s into the 70s, and may fall even lower at high elevations.

When to Go: May through September. June and July are especially popular with anglers, while sea kayakers and other pleasure boaters use the park from late spring through early fall. Bird-watching is best during the spring and fall migrations.

Facilities and Services: Most of Kachemak Bay State Park and Wilderness Park remains undeveloped, trailless wilderness, but several visitor facilities are concentrated in the Halibut Cove–Leisure Lake area, along the park's western border. They include a staffed ranger station (summer only), boat dock, 6 campgrounds (with pit toilets and fire rings), and 2 public-use cabins equipped with wooden bunks, table, and chairs. Open from May 15 to September 15, the cabins (up to three more are planned) may be reserved up to 6 months in advance. They sleep up to six people and have a maximum stay of 5 nights; check for updated cost information. A district office, which serves as the park's primary visitor-contact point, is at MP 168.5 of the Sterling Highway, just outside Homer. More than 20 guides, charter outfits, and air- or water-taxi services have permits to operate in the park; a list is available from the district office. Just outside the park's boundaries and on private inholdings within it are several wilderness lodges, as well as the tiny fishing and arts community of Halibut Cove, which has a restaurant, bed-and-breakfasts, and arts-and-crafts galleries.

Activities: Fishing and boating are most popular. Other coastal activities include clam digging, camping, picnicking, crabbing, beachcombing, photography, scuba diving, waterfowl hunting, berry picking, and wildlife viewing. Backcountry activities are hiking, skiing, backpacking, glacier travel, mountaineering, and hunting.

Hiking: The park has nearly 25 miles of interconnected trails, accessible from seven trailheads. Individual trails range from 1 to 5½ miles and vary from easy to strenuous. Two popular trails are the 3½-mile Grewingk Glacier Trail, an easy hike over flat terrain, and the steeper, 2-mile-long Alpine Ridge Trail. Trail guides are available from the district office.

For More Information: Phone the Alaska State Parks office in Homer, (907) 235-7024, or Soldotna, (907) 262-5581. Or write to the Division of Parks Kenai Area Office, P.O. Box 1247, Soldotna, AK 99669. For details on the public-use cabins, contact the Kenai Area Office, or the Department of Natural Resources' Public Information Center, P.O. Box 107005, Anchorage, AK 99510-7005; (907) 269-8400. Information on lodging and transportation can be obtained by contacting Homer Chamber of Commerce, P.O. Box 541, Homer, AK 99603; (907) 235-7740.

27

PADDLING WITH PORPOISES

▲ A harbor porpoise rolls through the placid waters of Berger Bay, along the western coastline of Nuka Island.

P*ffff*. Pause. *Pffff*.

I'd heard this sound my first night at Nuka Island and thought—hoped—it might be a sea mammal. Maybe even a whale. But I couldn't locate its source and eventually decided it must be waves lapping on the shore somewhere. Or my mind playing tricks. Tonight, on an evening paddle across glassy, tranquil Berger Bay, I hear it again: *Pffff . . . pffff*. Over there, by Berger Island.

I paddle slowly toward the sound and spot what looks like a wake. Then, a hundred yards away, maybe less, I see a curved back and dorsal fin gently break the water and disappear. And another. I count two, three animals. Not large. Not whales. They're harbor porpoises, also known as common porpoises.

Shivers running through me, I paddle closer. How close should I go? I don't want to scare them off. The sea otters and harbor seals I'd seen along Nuka Island had all been wary, easily spooked. For good reasons. The region's otters are hunted by Natives for their pelts, and seals are sometimes illegally shot or otherwise harassed by commercial fishermen. But the porpoises are different. They circle me, their dark bluish gray backs and fins rhythmically rolling in and out of the water. They seem to be everywhere. To my left, then my right. Behind. In front. Sometimes a quarter-mile away, sometimes 30 feet—or 20. Occasionally they snort and splash, in preparation for deeper dives. But mostly they cut the water with no perceptible sound, except their breathing. *Pffff . . . pffff . . . pffff*.

Smallest of the cetaceans (which include dolphins,

porpoises, and whales), *Phocoena phocoena* is widely distributed throughout the Pacific and one of only two kinds of porpoise to frequent Alaska's coastal waters (the other being the Dall porpoise). The species' loud breaths have prompted some less-than-charming nicknames—"herring hog," "puffing pig," and "sea pig"—but in my time with them, I fail to understand the porcine connection.

The porpoises swim alone or in small groups of two or three, often following each other in line. It's nearly impossible to get an accurate count of their numbers because they're constantly changing direction, diving, and reappearing where I don't expect them. Though at times I think there must be 15 or 20 of them, my best guess is 6 to 8 animals. That fits with what's known about harbor porpoises; they usually travel in small, matriarchal-dominated pods of 2 to 10 animals. More rarely they congregate in herds of 100 or more, to feed on schools of herring, cod, shrimp, or squid.

Once it's clear they're not intimidated, I wonder how close they'll approach. Will they bump the kayak, somehow upset it, knock it over, even in play? But these are small animals that only occasionally reach 4 feet long or weigh more than 130 pounds. And they're not aggressive toward humans. Any initial anxieties dissipate, giving way to joy and curiosity.

How do they perceive me and the kayak? As some sort of floating debris? Or do they connect me with other humans they've met? Harbor porpoises are known for approaching boats, though they rarely jump clear of the water or surface long enough for photographs. "They have no fear of humans, and they like to interact with vessels," Ron Morris of the National Marine Fisheries Service tells me later. "We're not sure whether they feel that boats provide shelter for small fish that they feed on or if they're simply curious. But it's a common occurrence for them to follow boats, sometimes for hours."

And what are they doing as they roll and dive? Feeding? Playing? Looking for food? Morris has no doubt: "Porpoises are much more active when they're feeding; they wouldn't have hung around. They were just lollygaggin' around, playing with you, having fun."

The pleasure is mine, as well, on this August evening. It's an unexpected treat to be paddling among porpoises. None of them nudge the boat or come close enough to touch, though Morris later assures me, "with harbor porpoises, it's possible you could have patted them on the head." There is, however, one brief encounter that will stay with me always. After 30 minutes, two of the porpoises roll directly in front of me. One surfaces 30 feet away. Then 15. *"Omygosh,"* I whisper aloud in amazement. It's coming right at me. What's it going to do?

What it does is swim right under the kayak, a distinct though shadowy apparition 5 or 6 feet below. For the first time I see the porpoise's entire form—the round head, squat body, triangular dorsal fin, dark flippers and tail—as it spurts past. My heart is pounding at this small miracle. Feeling blessed, I smile.

The porpoises come and go, sometimes disappearing for 5 or 10 minutes. Their first prolonged departure is accompanied by a large splash, and my imagination again takes flight; I wonder if they've been chased away by some larger ocean predator. Perhaps the black waters below me now hide a killer whale or a shark, both of which prey on harbor porpoises. How would a shark perceive my black-bottomed kayak? But the fears subside when the porpoises return, backs rolling as before. I stay in their company until almost 9:30 P.M., when fading light prompts my return to camp.

I'll see porpoises twice more before I leave Nuka Island, once a solitary animal, the other time a pair. But we're headed in opposite directions; and though I stop, hoping for renewed play, the porpoises continue on their way.

WOOD-TIKCHIK 2

WOOD-TIKCHIK STATE PARK

THE LONE RANGER AND AMERICA'S LARGEST STATE PARK

Rolling out of a sleeping bag stretched across his living room rug, Dan Hourihan gets a pot of coffee brewing, steps into the bathroom for his morning shower, and, by 9 A.M., begins his day's work. Hourihan's combination living room/bedroom now becomes his office. Amid the TV and well-worn easy chairs sit a desk, computer terminal, photocopying and fax machines, filing system, telephone, single sideband radio, and shelves stacked with books. Additional equipment and gear are stored in adjacent supply rooms.

Without knowing Hourihan's line of work, a visitor would reasonably suspect that he runs a small-scale, low-budget operation. Low budget, yes; small scale, not at all.

Forty-six-year-old Hourihan manages Wood-Tikchik State Park, located in Alaska's Bristol Bay region, about 325 miles southwest of Anchorage. At 1.6 million acres, Wood-Tikchik is the nation's largest state park. It's also the most understaffed and underfunded. Created in 1978, Wood-Tikchik has essentially been a one-man operation since 1985, when Hourihan was named its chief—and only—ranger. Before then, it received no active management at all.

From day one, Hourihan has been forced to make do with a budget that's "damn close to nothing." In 1994, for example, Alaska State Parks gave him $37,500 in general funds—including his salary—to manage this ruggedly spectacular region (his total budget, including user fees, was $70,000). There's

◀ The Wood River Mountains are reflected in Lake Kulik on a sunny August afternoon.
▲ Dan Hourihan, the "lone ranger" of Wood-Tikchik State Park

31

little money for park equipment or maintenance and none for other paid staff. But Hourihan prefers to see his funding dilemma as a blessing rather than a curse. "Being short-staffed and broke can be an advantage," he says with a smile. "It's forced me to reach out to the community and various park constituencies on a regular basis, to develop a support system and work with people. That's what parks are all about anyway: people."

To fill the staffing void, he recruits volunteers and whatever help he can muster from local residents and commercial operators. And to get equipment he couldn't otherwise afford, Hourihan bargains and barters. "What he accomplishes out there constantly amazes me," marvels Hourihan's wife, Pam, who playfully calls her husband "the scavenger." But scavenger isn't the sort of image one gets when meeting Dan, who at 5 feet 10 inches and 180 pounds is a muscular, wide-shouldered man with dark brown hair, neatly trimmed moustache, and dark eyes that often sparkle. A grizzly bear is more what comes to mind. Or, given his easy smile and playful demeanor, a teddy bear. It turns out he can be both.

Hourihan leaves his Eagle River home each spring to set up shop in Dillingham, a coastal fishing community of about 2,200 people that serves as the region's economic and transportation hub and is conveniently located near Wood-Tikchik's southern border. From late May through September, he's on duty 7 days a week, with only occasional "down days." He spends a third of his time in town, working out of cramped headquarters in a small building that he shares with the state's Department of Public Safety. The rest of the time—the best of times—Dan Hourihan roams Wood-Tikchik, where he serves as the "lone ranger" of America's largest and one of its most pristine state park units.

～∾～

ON HIS FIRST extended tour of Wood-Tikchik, Hourihan was struck by both the park's immensity and its incredible wild beauty. Here, in one unit, is 15 percent of the nation's entire state park acreage, all of it accessible only by boat, plane, or foot. No roads; no developed trails. The only land routes through the park are those regularly used by wildlife.

Despite its inland setting, Wood-Tikchik is a water-based park, dominated by—and named after—the Wood River and Tikchik lakes systems, each characterized by a series of large (up to 45 miles long) and interconnected clearwater lakes. The east-west-trending lakes bridge two distinct ecosystems. Their fjord-like western arms are dotted with islands and surrounded by the Wood River Mountains, a barely explored range of jagged spires and remote alpine valleys, while eastern shores are bounded by the tundra-dominated Nushagak Lowlands. Everything from grizzly bears and moose to porcupines, river otters, and owls inhabit the park's forests and tundra, but Wood-Tikchik is best known for its fish. Lakes and streams provide critical spawning grounds for five species of Pacific salmon and support healthy populations of several other fish species.

Recognized as one of Alaska's outstanding wilderness-recreation areas since the 1950s, the Wood-Tikchik region was once considered for inclusion in the National Parks System. Instead, its lands were picked by the state of Alaska in 1961, through rights granted by the statehood act. Proposals to protect the Wood-Tikchik drainages didn't end with the state's selection. "From 1963 on," Hourihan recalls, "there were discussions of preserving the area [as parkland]." However, local opposition—sparked by fears that traditional lifestyles and subsistence activities would be curtailed—delayed the park's creation until 1978. To rally public support, state officials agreed to establish a seven-person park management council, with five positions filled by local residents, to represent the communities of Dillingham, Koliganek, New Stuyahok, and Aleknagik, as well as the Bristol Bay Native Association (BBNA), which represents the region's Yupik, Aleut, and Athabascan peoples.

"The council's makeup gave some assurance that locals would have a large say in the park's management," Hourihan says. Similarly, the park's management priorities reflect local value systems. Its primary reasons for being are to protect critical fish and wildlife habitat *and* preserve traditional subsistence and recreational activities.

Wood-Tikchik State Park was virtually ignored for the first 6 years. No budget. No staff. No management plan. Finally, in 1984, state parks officials decided to assign a ranger to the park. Hourihan, then Chugach State Park's acting chief ranger, "absolutely loved Chugach." But he leaped at the chance to explore new horizons. "I was single then, so I didn't have the ties some other people did," he remembers. "And the idea of being the first ranger in the last big unstaffed park, either state or federal, was something I just couldn't resist."

Hourihan faced an enormous challenge: not only would he be Wood-Tikchik's first ranger, but he'd be the first ranger ever assigned to a park west of the Alaska Range, where most residents have an innate distrust of the "P word" and anyone wearing a uniform (whether park employees or police). And he was going there with minimal resources and connections. It was the perfect assignment for a former army counterintelligence agent with a flair for improvisation and network building.

Hourihan flew into Dillingham in February 1985 with a bare-bones budget and no supplies, except for the personal items he'd crammed into a pack and duffel. He set up headquarters in a corner of the Alaska Department of Fish and Game building and slept on the floor next to his "office"—a desk. (He finally got some "bunk space" in 1986 and the following year moved into the building he now shares with Public Safety.)

"Partly it was bad timing," he says. "We began to actively manage the park when state revenues from oil production were beginning to decline, so we didn't get any direct funding from the legislature. I had no money to speak of and no equipment. Luckily, Fish and Game was real supportive. Right from the start, we've enjoyed wonderful interagency cooperation."

Using his negotiating talents—and a $20,000 "donation" from Chugach State Park's budget—Hourihan soon began hitting up Fish and Game for needed equipment. Among his earliest acquisitions were surplus

BACKCOUNTRY CAMPING

▲ High-quality gear is a necessity for camping in Alaska.

When choosing a wilderness campsite, consider the following factors: a nearby source of water, good drainage, protection from high winds, the presence of game trails, tidal influences (along the coast), impact on fragile vegetation, and, in winter, avalanche paths. Before going into any area, check with the local ranger to learn specific guidelines and regulations and also get tips on possible campsites.

To avoid frustrations—or worse, emergencies—use high-quality backpacking and camping gear. Winter-like storms can occur at almost any time of year in Alaska, so pack a four-season tent (one that will withstand strong winds and persistent rains). Other must-have shelter items include adequate stakes, tie-down ropes, tent fly, ground cloth, and mosquito netting. Many tents come with vestibules, which offer additional space for gear plus a convenient place to cook in nasty weather. Never cook inside the tent itself, to avoid fire and asphyxiation. A tarp is nice to have, especially in wet weather. Bring a sleeping bag that's suitable for the worst weather you might encounter; in most of Alaska's alpine areas, summer nighttime lows may dip below freezing. Sleeping pads add cushioning and insulation. Always bring a backpacking stove, for boiling water and cooking meals.

Campers should practice leave-no-trace camping techniques to minimize damage to the environment. Bring litter bags and pack out *all* garbage. Avoid camping on fragile vegetation, which can be easily trampled and, in alpine areas, often takes years to recover. If possible, camp on gravel or already established and hardened sites. Keep a clean camp, and store your food so that wild animals won't be able to get it. Use biodegradable soaps and wash yourself, your clothes, and dishes at least 100 feet from water sources. Bring a trowel and dig 6- to 8-inch-deep cat holes for human waste, at least 100 feet from your camp, water sources, and trails. Burn or carry out toilet paper. Avoid building campfires; Alaska's state parks generally require campers to build fires in designated pits or on gravel bars and sandy beaches. If you do build a fire, place it on dirt or gravel, use only dead and downed wood, and be sure the fire is extinguished before you leave.

When traveling, don't shortcut switchbacks. This creates new trails and destroys vegetation unnecessarily. When crossing trailless areas—particularly tundra—fan out instead of walking single-file, again to avoid trampling vegetation.

items—everything from tents to a powerboat—left over from a defunct wildlife-research study. Staffing offered another challenge. "It was painfully clear from the beginning that one ranger cannot adequately patrol 1.6 million acres, so what we've done is build an unpaid staff," he says. "We've brought volunteerism to a fine art."

Over the years, volunteers have contributed several hundred thousand hours of "free" labor. The state provides the unpaid staffers with "room"—usually a tent—and meals. In return, they conduct surveys, do maintenance work, participate in fish and wildlife research programs, offer information to visitors, and, perhaps most important of all, provide a high-profile backcountry presence.

While equipment and staffing needs demanded innovative solutions, regional attitudes presented an even greater challenge. To local residents, Hourihan's arrival signaled undesirable change, the start of a new era with great potential for unwanted rules and regulations.

"In the beginning, there was a lot of apprehension," says Dugan Nielsen, a one-quarter Aleut who's employed by BBNA and serves on the park's management council. "There are some significant hunting and fishing grounds in the park that locals have relied on for years, and people wondered how their subsistence lifestyle would be affected. People weren't sure what to expect from this new guy coming in here."

Acceptance came grudgingly at first. Hourihan received several threats his first summer, including one while out on patrol. He'd cited two intoxicated local residents for fishing without a license and exceeding the catch limit, when one of the fishermen pulled a knife and threatened to plunge it into Hourihan's inflatable raft (he didn't get a jet boat until 1986). Looking the man straight in the eye, the powerfully built ranger responded in a calm, steady voice, "You do that and things are gonna happen real fast." End of threat and start of no-nonsense law-enforcement reputation. Now, he says, "Some of the people who gave me the most trouble in the beginning are my biggest allies."

Hourihan also proved to be a consensus builder, a friend. Rather than carrying an aura of authority,

"Ranger Dan" brought an easy smile, an open mind, and a spirit of compromise. "I'm only two eyes and two ears in the biggest state park in the nation," he says. "If I didn't remember who I worked for—the public—I'd be very ineffective. My experience has been, the more partnerships you can build, the better off you'll be."

Hourihan's willingness to share his ideas and listen to others won over most of the skeptics. "From the start, Dan made it clear that he wanted to work together with the people," says Nielsen. "He has the sort of personality that the job requires. He's very open and loves to talk; that removes any mystery about his role."

Pete Panarese, Alaska State Parks' chief of field operations and a longtime friend of Hourihan, agrees that his pal's "gift of gab" has served him well at Wood-Tikchik. But Panarese, whose life in many ways has paralleled Hourihan's—both attended the University of Maine, served in the army, and have worked in Alaska's State Parks System since the late 1970s—also stresses the importance of Hourihan's military training.

"Dan's skills were exactly what was needed to develop a successful program at Wood-Tikchik," Panarese says. "His military background had taught him to be totally independent; he could move in and set up an operation with virtually no resources. That was critical for managing a 1½-million-acre park he hardly knew. Dan also realized it was critical to recruit and develop a network of allies, a 'source net,' if you will. He's culled support from all sorts of different groups: the Alaska Department of Fish and Game, BBNA, the [sportfishing] lodge owners. People believe in Dan and his program."

By the end of his first year, Hourihan knew he'd taken a major step toward becoming part of Dillingham's community. Several people came to the airport to see him off and gave him a going-away gift: strips of smoked salmon.

EARLY JUNE, the start of another summer season. Having tended to his most pressing in-town responsibilities,

Hourihan is taking his 21-foot aluminum jet boat, the *Silver Loon*, into the park on a 3-day patrol. Piled on board are several boxes of food and miscellaneous gear, to resupply three volunteers already stationed inside the park. And strapped to the boat's bow is a 5-by-5-by-7-foot yellow plastic septic tank. Hourihan has agreed to deliver it to Golden Horn Lodge, one of five fishing lodges built before Wood-Tikchik's creation and allowed, by state regulations, to operate on private inholdings within the park (two others are just outside its boundaries). Soon nicknamed the "yellow monster," the plastic tank forces him to stand on an ice chest while navigating upstream.

Among the many items he has scavenged from Fish and Game, the *Silver Loon* is one of Hourihan's most precious tools. Moored at Aleknagik Lake whenever he's in Dillingham, the boat provides easy and inexpensive access to all the Wood River system's major lakes. A second, smaller, jet boat is kept at Tikchik Lake for patrols within that system. (Because it's more remote and reasonably accessible only by floatplane, the Tikchik drainage is less often visited, both by park staff and others.)

Besides serving as Wood-Tikchik's primary transportation corridors and recreational playgrounds, the park's two lake systems provide critical fish and wildlife habitat. Both drainages are home to healthy populations of rainbow and lake trout, salmon, char, grayling, and pike, and together they serve as spawning grounds for up to 20 percent of Bristol Bay's annual sockeye return. Because its waters contain such a variety and abundance of species popular with anglers, the Wood-Tikchik area has long been recognized as one of Alaska's prime sport fisheries. Hundreds of fishermen from around the world visit the park each year from June through October. Most stay at the lodges that work its streams and lakes.

◄ Once used primarily by hunters and anglers, Wood-Tikchik State Park in recent years has attracted a growing number of kayakers and other boaters.

▲ Wood-Tikchik ranger Dan Hourihan pilots the *Silver Loon* across Lake Nerka.

such as poaching, littering, and wildlife harassment.

Among the most senior lodge owners is Bud Hodson, who has worked the Wood-Tikchik area since 1974, when he hired on at Royal Coachman Lodge; since 1986, he's owned and operated the Tikchik Narrows Lodge. A lot has changed in 22 years. The number of lodges, and consequently the fishing pressure on rainbows and salmon, has increased substantially. Lodge rates have jumped from $1,500 a week in 1979 to more than $4,000 a week in 1996. And since the mid-1980s, there's been a park ranger to deal with.

"Things could have been difficult if we'd gotten a 'cop' ranger, one who goes strictly by the book and [thinks he] knows what's best for everyone," says Hodson, former chairman of Alaska's Board of Fisheries. "We were lucky to get Dan. He's very smart; he knew he was coming into our world, and he brought minimal bureaucracy into it. He's never been standoff-ish, and has made it clear he's here to work with us."

—∞—

HOURIHAN'S JOURNEY to Wood-Tikchik State Park began four decades ago in downtown Boston. Enraptured at an early age by wild places and animals, he often escaped into the outdoors through books and magazines. "I lived in that world vicariously," he recalls. "The North Woods and the mountains had a special allure."

As a 13-year-old paper carrier, he won a contest sponsored by the *Cleveland Plain Dealer*. His prize: a 2-week visit to the Colorado Rockies, including 7 days at a dude ranch. "After that trip," he says, "I had no doubts that I'd end up a western boy, either in, or close to, the mountains." Before moving west, however, Hourihan returned east to finish high school and attend the University of Maine, where he majored in English, played football, joined a fraternity, and, best of all, began to explore the North Woods. It was, he says, a period of self-realization. Finally, he could structure his life to allow ample time for what mattered most: the woods, the mountains . . . nature.

Those lodges serve two important functions. Through commercial user fees, they contribute substantially to Wood-Tikchik's available funds; in 1994, for example, commercial operators—fishing lodges, air-taxi operators, hunting guides, and outfitters—accounted for $32,000. And because lodge owners have a stake in Wood-Tikchik's health, they help deter illegal activities

FISHING THE PAK

The rainbow chasers begin arriving just after 8 A.M. A floatplane from Crystal Creek Lodge is the first to land, followed by aircraft from Tikchik Narrows and Bristol Bay lodges. During the next 10 hours, the lodges' guides will introduce their clients to some of the best rainbow trout fishing in the world.

The river they've come to fish is the Agulukpak—or simply the "Pak"—located about 40 air miles north of Dillingham. Less than 3 miles long, the Pak links Beverley and Nerka Lakes within the Wood River system. Each July and August, this small clearwater stream serves as an avenue for nearly a half million sockeye salmon bound for spawning grounds in Beverley and Kulik Lakes. Following the sockeyes are large numbers of rainbow trout—as many as 2,000 per river mile, according to state sport-fish studies—which gorge themselves on salmon eggs when spawning begins.

Competition between guided angling parties, though generally friendly, can become intense. Seven lodges are located within, or near, Wood-Tikchik State Park. And all fish the Pak on a regular basis. "The Pak is *the* fishing spot within the park," says ranger Dan Hourihan. "It gets the most use, by far, of any place."

Until the salmon spawn, trout feed on a variety of prey, and each of the lodges has its own "secret" fly patterns for catching Pak rainbows. But all guided parties use similar strategies to locate the trout. Wearing neoprene chest waders and literally hanging on to their 14- to 16-foot motorized skiffs, guides walk behind the boats, which go down the stream stern-first, and steer their clients through the most productive fishing holes.

The guides begin their runs near Beverley's outlet, just above the first set of riffles and holes. There they anchor up, explain the techniques to be employed, and offer a quickie course in fly-fishing drift-style. Because of the Pak's popularity with local lodges and the guides' high success rate, only catch-and-release, fly-fishing methods are permitted. Fishing expertise is helpful, but hardly a prerequisite, because the preferred method is to simply flip the fly upstream and let it drift with the current. To further aid their clients, many guides also use "strike indicators," small phosphorescent orange cork-like bobbers. Whenever clients (two per boat is the norm) hook into a fish, the guides anchor their boat, then help land the rainbow, remove the hook, and release it.

The anglers normally drift less than a mile, then return to the head of the river; by day's end, they may make a dozen or more runs. With a half dozen or more boats working the river, it's not unusual for hundreds of rainbows to be caught; many measure 20 inches or more and weigh up to 7 pounds.

Largely because of its remote location and, perhaps, its relative anonymity, the Pak has traditionally been fished almost exclusively by lodge customers. Steered to the best fishing holes and aided by experts who work the river daily, guided clients have a clear advantage over unguided anglers, but of course they pay for that advantage: the going rate at most fishing lodges in the Wood-Tikchik region is more than $4,000 per week.

▼ **Fishing the Pak for rainbows**

While at Maine, Hourihan also discovered a kindred spirit in Pete Panarese. Classmates, frat brothers, and climbing partners, they spent as much time as possible in the mountains and laid the foundation of a lasting friendship. After college, both men joined the army. Panarese left after 4 years; Hourihan stayed in for 6. While on leave in September 1973, he visited Panarese, then stationed at Fort Richardson, near Anchorage. They hiked up the East Fork of Chugach State Park's Eklutna River, where the tundra was ablaze with autumn's reds and yellows. Beneath a crystal-clear sky, Hourihan spent his first night in Alaska's backcountry. "It was magical," he says, "but nature has always been like that for me; it's a very important component of my psychological and spiritual life."

Four years later, Hourihan joined Panarese on Chugach's staff. Over the next 7 years he held nearly every available position except park superintendent. Then, in 1985, he got the Wood-Tikchik job. "By ending up at Chugach we'd both realized our aspirations," Panarese says. "The only difference is that I progressed into management, while Dan chose to stay in the field."

Leaving Eagle River each May isn't as easy as it used to be. Not when a family gets left behind. Married since 1988, Dan and Pam Hourihan have four children, 6 to 20 years old: Ian, Ryli, Katherine, and Courtney.

"I like to joke that I'm a 'military wife' for part of every year," says Pam, who grew up in Anchorage and, ironically, spent many childhood summers in Dillingham, where her grandfather owned a flight service. "I'm reasonably content with staying at home while Dan's out in the field. We stay in touch a lot, but the two youngest are at an age where they're missing their father, and I always do.

"Dan has talked about coming into town and taking a full-time desk job, but that's not him [although he spends his winters in Anchorage, doing administrative work]. I remember once when Dan was thinking about applying for a superintendent position. We were in the park, sitting in the *Silver Loon* and watching a sunset together. The mountains, the lakes, the sky—it was all so beautiful. I said, 'You know, it would be a shame for you to take that job. This is what you love.' "

Panarese would agree. Still, he's constantly amazed at the sacrifices Hourihan makes to run the show at Wood-Tikchik: "Dan has done this at considerable personal expense, yet he's never pushed [the Division of Parks] about fair compensation. He's taken a very altruistic approach. But one of these days Dan is gonna say, 'Enough. Time to move on.' "

Hourihan himself sometimes wonders when that day will come. But for now he's willing to make the necessary sacrifices, while guiding the park through its formative years. There's still much to be accomplished. Perhaps the biggest challenge is that of private-property inholdings. Local Native residents have claimed more than 100 parcels of land within the park's boundaries, through the 1906 Native Allotment Act. Averaging 80 acres, the parcels are scattered throughout the park, many of them in key habitat locations. If they are developed without regard for the park's values, the character of Wood-Tikchik could be irreparably harmed.

Emphasizing "it's not a Native issue, it's a land-use issue," Hourihan has worked tirelessly with claimants, members of Wood-Tikchik's management council, and representatives of BBNA to craft a strategy that's fair to all parties. Dugan Nielsen describes negotiations as "a very delicate balancing act" and commends the ranger for his efforts to find a win-win solution.

Hourihan, meanwhile, remains hopeful that "we can negotiate a compromise that protects park values and the public's interest, while giving people what they're entitled to. The final outcome of this issue will postdate me; we're looking 20, 30 years down the line. But I'm the one who's been asked to steward the park at this time. It would be tragic for me, personally, to walk through Dillingham 20 or 30 years from now and have people say, 'Whatever happened? Remember how it used to be?' As chief ranger, my greatest personal and professional concern is the present and future well-being of Wood-Tikchik State Park."

▲ **Western columbine**

IF YOU GO

Getting There: Located in the Bristol Bay region, about 325 miles southwest of Anchorage, Wood-Tikchik State Park is accessible only by plane, boat, or foot in summer. Most recreational visitors fly into the park using air-taxi services based in Dillingham, which in turn is served by daily commercial airline flights to and from Anchorage. Once in the park, the easiest way to get around is by boat, via the Wood River and Tikchik lakes systems; folding kayaks and inflatable rafts or canoes are popular.

Weather: Generally cool and wet. Average midsummer daytime highs and lows are 65°F and 45°F. Strong winds out of the southeast or southwest often blow across the park's east-west-trending lakes. Stormy weather may delay arrival or departure by several days.

When to Go: The main visitor season, for both anglers and boaters, begins in early to mid-June and lasts through mid-September. Most recreational and trophy hunting occurs from August through October. Winter use is rare, except by local residents.

Facilities and Services: Managed as a wild area, Wood-Tikchik has limited visitor facilities. There are no maintained trails, and only four "developed" camping areas—with a total of 12 tent sites—have been established, though backcountry camping is allowed throughout the park. Most developed sites are "primitive," without running water, latrines, or other amenities. A small campground (with latrine) and a ranger cabin have been established near the mouth of Lake Beverley. Those seeking greater luxury may wish to stay at one of the region's fishing lodges. A list of lodges and other commercial services can be obtained from the Alaska State Parks System.

Activities: Fishing, kayaking, rafting, mountain climbing, wildlife viewing, hiking, and hunting.

Hiking: Cross-country hiking and backpacking are possible, but because there are no trails, map-reading and route-finding skills are essential. Travel is difficult at lower elevations, because of dense alder–willow thickets, and throughout most of the park, considerable bushwhacking is necessary to reach more open alpine tundra.

For More Information: From May 15 through October 1, contact Chief Ranger Dan Hourihan, c/o Wood-Tikchik State Park, P.O. Box 3022, Dillingham, AK 99576; (907) 842-2375. The remainder of the year, contact Hourihan c/o Wood-Tikchik State Park, 3601 C Street, Suite 1200, Anchorage, AK 99503; (907) 269-8698. Also recommended is *A Backcountry Naturalist's Guide to Wood-Tikchik State Park*, by Philip Caswell.

▼ **Getting started: Backcountry travelers assemble their Klepper kayak on the shore of Lake Kulik.**

FLOATING THROUGH WOOD-TIKCHIK

▲ Californian Glenn Ward paddles his kayak across mirror-smooth Lake Beverley during a 2-week trip through Wood-Tikchik State Park.

The Wind River, by most river-running standards, is an easy float. This 2-mile, clear-water mountain stream is a mixture of Class I and II white water. Simple stuff. But flying over the Wind on a mid-August afternoon, I don't see "easy" or "simple." I see boulders and one short but intense stretch of rapids. I see calamity.

White-water anxieties soon give way to the calming influence of darker, more tranquil waters. Below us is Lake Kulik, the starting point for most paddling expeditions through Wood-Tikchik State Park. Long and narrow, Kulik stretches serpent-like across 20 miles of wilderness. Deepest at its west end, becoming ever more shallow to the east, the lake fills a glacially carved trench and connects disparate landscapes.

At Kulik's eastern tail end are tundra, marshes, and other wetlands. From out of this lowland muck and mire, the lake undulates westward through alder–willow thickets and forested foothills, until its head opens into the Wood River Mountains. The range isn't grand by Alaskan standards—the park's tallest peak is 5,026-foot Mount Waskey—but it's wild, remote, and rugged.

Rising into blue-sky heavens, the park's high country seizes my imagination. I'd love to walk its bare-rock ridgelines, camp in alpine meadows, sit atop a granite spire. They're so inviting from the air, these mountains, but they're also beyond my reach. Like nearly all Wood-Tikchik visitors, I'm unwilling to do what's necessary to reach the open heights, unwilling to fight through thick brush and pick my way through forested hillsides while hauling a 50- or 60-pound pack. Instead of a cross-country trek, I'll explore the park by boat. This is the usual way people travel through Wood-Tikchik, and the most sensible way, we've been told.

My traveling companions, Dulcy Boehle and Glenn Ward, and I have brought two Kleppers for our journey down the Wood River system. Intended for ocean paddling, these folding kayaks are stable, durable boats, but they're also heavy and not highly maneuverable. They're not the best of river boats, in other words.

From Lake Kulik, it's possible to paddle all the way to Dillingham—the jumping-off spot for most Wood-Tikchik trips—110 river and lake miles away. But we've instead decided on a leisurely 2-week, 45-mile trip from Kulik to Lake Nerka. That will give us plenty of time to explore, relax, and sit out stormy weather. For most of our visit we'll be paddling across lakes, but we also have 6 miles of river travel. People who know the area have assured us that the streams can be floated without great difficulty, even by paddlers like us, with no river-running experience.

After camping 3 days on Kulik's north shore, we cross to the lake's outlet to face our first challenge: a short but intimidating chute of churning white water.

Dulcy, the most experienced kayaker, goes first and cruises through. Next, Glenn and I. A moment of panic, and it's over. In a side eddy, we celebrate with cheers. Then, bolstered by our early success, we push downstream. Our passage becomes a dream-like blur, a strange blend of fast-forward and slow-motion images. Barely in control, we follow the current through shallow riffles, past sweepers and submerged boulders. Prolonged periods of nervousness are followed by brief interludes of relief and exhilaration. Gradually my confidence builds. And then we run into a boulder.

Glenn, sitting up front, spots the barely submerged rock seconds before we hit and yells, "*Boulder ahead, boulder . . .*" Our bow skims past, but the stern swings left and we crunch broadside into the barrel-sized rock. I hear, and feel, the Klepper's rubber hull scraping against the boulder's top; it seems the bottom must be tearing apart.

For a few seconds we're hung up on the rock, then somehow we swivel off, still upright. Back in the water, the Klepper seems in one piece, but we pull over to shore to look for damage. Once out of the fast-moving current, Glenn and I feel water sloshing around our boots. Quickly, we remove our gear (protected inside waterproof bags) and turn the boat over. We've been lucky: the hull damage is minor. There's one small circular gash and several punctures. Using duct tape and sealant we repair the torn bottom. The Klepper's wooden frame has also been damaged, but with the duct tape, we're able to mend the cracked pieces.

There would be other panicked moments, other boulder fields, other white-water rapids. But nothing like that first day on the Wind River. There would also be winds of 50 miles per hour or more, pounding rain, 3- and 4-foot whitecaps on the lakes. But early on, we agree to never push the weather. Our motto: "When in doubt, sit it out." And despite our initial traumas, kayaks prove to be an ideal vehicle for traveling through this "land of lakes."

43

During its first 7 years of being, Wood-Tikchik almost exclusively attracted anglers and hunters. But since the mid-1980s, a growing number of people have come to explore its river-lake systems, see its wildlife and scenery, and experience its solitude. Visits by waterborne adventurers—mainly kayakers and rafters—have grown steadily since 1985. Despite this "boom," it's still possible to travel for days in some of the more remote waters and not meet another group of people.

The park's most popular fly-in float trip is the 85-mile journey from Lake Kulik to Alegnagik, a Yupik

▼ Monkshood is found in Alaska's woodland and alpine meadows.

Eskimo village east of Dillingham. Though it can be done in less than a week, ranger Dan Hourihan recommends at least 10 days to 2 weeks, so paddlers can explore the park and not feel pressured to travel during stormy weather.

While streams connecting the Wood River lakes are relatively easy floats, the more northerly and remote Tikchik lakes system has white-water stretches that demand portages. Most parties begin their journeys at Nishlik Lake and float the shallow, fast-moving Tikchik River to Tikchik Lake, a distance of about 60 miles. Paddlers seeking further adventure can cross Tikchik Lake and travel another 40 to 50 miles to the village of Koliganek (outside the park), via the Nuyakuk River. The upper Nuyakuk demands great caution, and Hourihan advises river runners to portage around both the Class III and IV Nuyakuk Rapids and the Class V-plus Nuyakuk Falls.

⚬⚬⚬

WE REACH THE AGULUKPAK RIVER, the last stream we'll float, on August 18, our ninth day in the park. We've come 27 miles in all, 12 miles today across Lake Beverley. After 2 days of rain and high winds, the weather has turned calm and sunny, with temperatures in the 70s.

The Agulukpak—"Pak" for short—is a busy place by Wood-Tikchik standards. Guided anglers visit daily, and boaters often stop to camp. Because it's heavily used and centrally located, Hourihan has established a backcountry outpost here, run by park volunteers who keep track of visitor trends, answer questions, do field studies, and "maintain a park presence." There's also a primitive campground here.

One volunteer, Phil Caswell, is compiling *A Backcountry Naturalist's Guide to Wood-Tikchik State Park*. Caswell's primary interest is botany, and he's identified hundreds of plant species in Wood-Tikchik. But he's also compiled a list of the park's birds and mammals. Though relatively little birding has been done, more than 140 species have been identified. We've seen lots of birds but few mammals during our first 9 days. Porcupines, squirrels, beavers. That's been something of a surprise, and a disappointment, but typical of the Wood River system, where dense shoreline brush limits visibility. Caswell, who has spent months in the park's backcountry, cautions, "Wild as Wood-Tikchik may be, its animals and less-common plants are frustratingly elusive. Feel lucky whenever you see a beaver or a moose . . . and rejoice if you see a lynx, wolverine, or wolf!" Caribou, in recent years, have proved a notable exception to that rule of elusiveness. The Mulchatna herd has grown to nearly 200,000 animals, and they can now be found throughout the lakes systems.

We stay at the campground 2 days, then begin the final leg of our journey: down the Pak and across Lake Nerka. With advice from park volunteers, we negotiate the Agulukpak's boulder "gardens" and Class II riffles with minimal distress. Winds and rough water on Nerka force us to camp at the Pak's mouth, but by morning the lake has calmed enough to paddle the 6 miles to Middle Island, where we set up camp and settle in for another day and a half of R and R. Our first evening at Middle Island is wonderfully peaceful. Once the floatplane traffic has stopped for the night, there's a pervading stillness, a silence that's only occasionally broken by the shrieks of gulls and the haunting songs of loons. Sitting on the beach, listening to the loons and looking at lake and mountains and sky, we become immersed in the wildness of the place.

Middle Island is 9 miles short of our designated pickup spot, but it's where our trip ends. The day we've set aside for our final paddle is clear, but westerly gales turn the lake into a whitecapped froth. Keeping to our motto, we stay put.

▲ Wood-Tikchik volunteers play cards at the Agulukpak ranger cabin.

August 24 brings another weather change: sunny and dead calm. Perfect traveling weather, a day late. We'd scheduled an early morning pickup, so all we can do is wait for pilot Mike Harder, who'll now have to search for us. Thankfully, he too understands there's no sense taking chances with the weather. As morning passes into afternoon, at least a half dozen planes fly overhead, none Mike's. Just as we're resigning ourselves to another night in the park—and missed airline connections to Anchorage—a plane buzzes the island. Our ride has arrived.

CHUGACH 3

CHUGACH STATE PARK
WILDERNESS AT THE EDGE OF TOWN

Friday afternoon, late April. End of a busy work week—so busy that I've kept myself sequestered indoors, despite 6 straight days of bright blue skies, glorious sunshine, and springtime warmth. Today, finally, I leave my hurried, too-much-to-do city life and head for the hills. After too long away, I return to Anchorage's backyard wilderness, Chugach State Park. Back to visit an old friend: 3,550-foot Flattop Mountain.

Huffing and puffing, sweating heavily in 50-degree air, I slog my way up Flattop's still snowy trail. Following bootprints of other hikers through mud and slush, I experience a strong sense of déjà vu. The feeling, however, seems less eerie than inevitable: I have indeed passed this way many times before. Enough times that my feet have almost memorized the trail's twists and turns.

Within 45 minutes, I'm on the mountain's top and gazing across a huge chunk of Southcentral Alaska: 120 miles to the north, the skyline is dominated by the Alaska Range's twin giants, Denali and Sultana, while nearly 100 miles to the southwest is Mount Redoubt's volcanic cone. More immediately below me are the Anchorage Bowl and Cook Inlet. And along the eastern horizon, stretching south to north, are the Chugach Mountains, alpine wilderness on the eastern doorstep of Anchorage, Alaska's largest city, a quarter million strong and growing.

A brisk wind usually roars across Flattop's summit, but today the air is

◄ An early summer view of the Chugach Mountains, looking northeast toward Williwaw Lakes (middle left in the picture).
▲ A hiker stands on Flattop Mountain's still-snowy summit in April.

calm. It's so still, so quiet, that I can hear the snowpack melt: faint slumping noises reflect audible shifts in crystal-liquid interfaces, as snow yields to water. No other sound but my breathing until a flock of honking geese flies overhead. Once the geese pass, there's not a creature in sight. No Dall sheep. No ravens or ptarmigan. No people. All the solitude I could ever want.

As afternoon gives way to evening, other hikers join me on top. Later, returning to the trailhead, I meet at least a dozen people bound for the summit. There's a busyness to the mountain now, signaling the approach of summer. Within a month or two, such warm and sunny days will lure crowds of people to Flattop. By September, 8,000 to 10,000 people—preschoolers and senior citizens, solitary hill runners and entire families, curious tourists and hard-core mountaineers—will have scrambled up its trails.

In a state with 19 peaks above 14,000 feet and 17 of the nation's 20 highest mountains, Flattop is a mere bump, an ordinary hill. But locally this sawed-off mountain has an extraordinary allure. Less than 15 miles from downtown Anchorage and visible throughout the city, Flattop is easy to find, easy to reach, and, as mountains go, easy to climb. From the main trailhead, it's only 1½ miles and 1,350 feet in elevation gain to the summit. And in summer no climbing expertise is needed: the ascent is more of a strenuous hike, with some rock scrambling necessary near the top. (That's not to say the mountain can't pose dangers; a handful of people have died on its slopes.) Most people can be up and back in 2 or 3 hours. Nearly all of Anchorage's residents, it seems, have climbed Flattop, or at least tried. And enough have succeeded to make it easily the most-climbed mountain in Alaska.

For many, Flattop is the initial lure to the 495,000-acre "accessible wilderness" east of Anchorage. Established in 1970, Chugach State Park encloses the western edge of the Chugach Mountains, a 300-mile-long coastal range that arcs from Cook Inlet almost to the Canadian border.

Measured in absolute numbers, the Chugach Range is not especially grand; its tallest peak, Mount Marcus Baker (east of the park), is only 13,176 feet high, nearly 1½ miles shorter than Denali. But measured from base to summit, the Chugach is Alaska's second-highest coastal range. These mountains also support 8,200 square miles of glacial ice, more than a quarter of the state's total.

Though neither as high nor as remote as its eastern extension, the western Chugach, beyond its civilized fringes, is a wild and rugged mountain kingdom, rich with wildlife, jagged spires, forested valleys, rushing streams, tundra meadows, and alpine lakes. Within Chugach's park boundaries are 155 peaks—the highest is 8,005-foot Bashful—dozens of glaciers, 2,000 Dall sheep, 500 mountain goats, 400 black bears, 300 moose, 25 grizzlies, and at least 2 wolf packs. A place of expansive alpine tundra, fringed by boreal forests and coastal waters, the park is seasonally inhabited by nearly 50 species of mammals—from orca whales and harbor porpoises to little brown bats and five species of shrews—100 species of birds, 9 species of fish, and 1 amphibian species, the wood frog.

Largely unknown outside the state, the park attracts more than a million visitors annually, 90 percent of them Alaskans, and is regarded by many locals as Anchorage's "crown jewel."

"Chugach State Park has become part of the fabric of life in Anchorage; it's one of the best things we've got going for us," says former State Parks System director Chip Dennerlein. "The character of the city and community would be dramatically different without the mountains and the recreational opportunities possible in the park. It adds to the quality of life, no question."

Anchorage economist Gunnar Knapp once determined that nearly three-fifths of Alaska's population lives within 40 miles of the park. And those nearby residents use the park heavily, in myriad ways: camping, picnicking, berry picking, taking photographs, viewing wildlife, backpacking, hiking, sightseeing, rock and ice climbing, horseback riding, mountain biking, hang gliding, boating, fishing, hunting, snowmobiling, snowshoeing, mushing, and skiing. Yet most people never

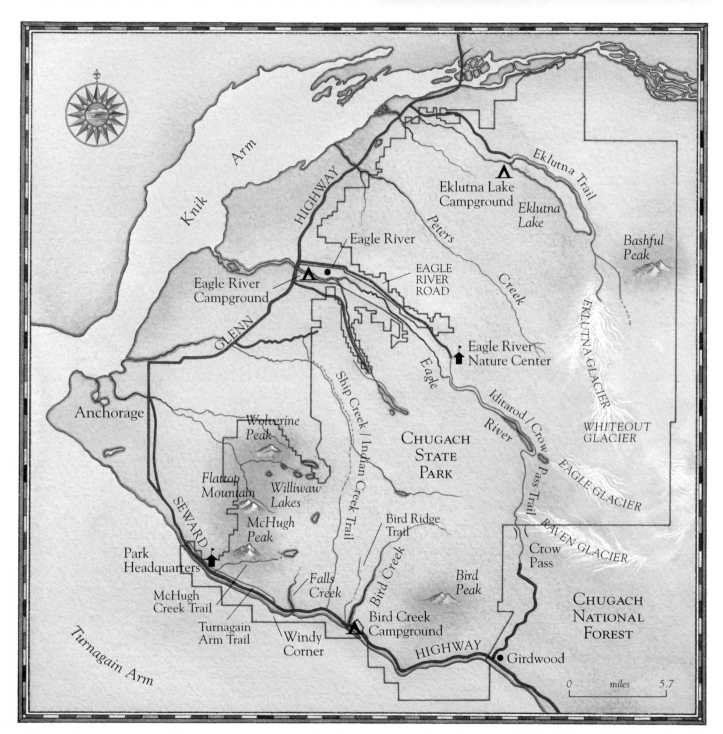

Knik Arm

Eklutna Trail

HIGHWAY

Eklutna Lake
Campground

Eklutna
Lake

Peters

Bashful
Peak

Eagle River

EAGLE
RIVER
ROAD

Eagle River
Campground

Creek

EKLUTNA GLACIER

GLENN

Eagle River
Nature Center

Eagle

WHITEOUT
GLACIER

Anchorage

Wolverine
Peak

Iditarod / Crow

River

CHUGACH
STATE
PARK

EAGLE GLACIER

Ship Creek / Indian Creek Trail

Flattop
Mountain

Williwaw
Lakes

Pass Trail

RAVEN GLACIER

SEWARD

McHugh
Peak

Bird Ridge
Trail

Crow
Pass

Park
Headquarters

Falls
Creek

Bird Creek

Bird
Peak

CHUGACH
NATIONAL
FOREST

McHugh
Creek Trail

Bird Creek
Campground

Turnagain
Arm Trail

Windy
Corner

HIGHWAY

Girdwood

Turnagain Arm

0   miles   5.7

▲ Two members of the Falls Creek Band, a Dall sheep ewe and her lamb, peer from behind a rocky ledge in the cliffs overlooking the Seward Highway.

venture more than a mile or two into the park and probably no more than a few dozen have explored its most remote ridges and valleys.

~~~

ON A WARM and sunny July morning, Shawn Lyons nimbly hops from boulder to boulder while crossing a talus pile near Williwaw Lakes. It's the sort of summer day that's perfect for picnics or napping in grassy meadows, but in keeping with Lyons's backcountry philosophy, we're moving fast. No lounging among the wildflowers today. "A lot of people say to stop and smell the roses, but I think you remember more by traveling quickly. It forces you to pay attention," he explains. "Having a goal helps keep a person awake."

Our goal today is an 18-mile circumnavigation of 4,455-foot Wolverine Peak, one of 16 Chugach Front

Range mountains visible from Anchorage. This is Lyons's sixth trip around Wolverine, my first. He's cut back on his engines to accommodate my slower pace, but still must occasionally stop and wait. In 8½ hours of hiking, we'll see more Dall sheep (a half dozen) than people, hear more raven calls than human voices.

A 40-something classical guitarist and university music teacher, Lyons has the sinewy build (6 feet tall, 145 pounds) and graceful stride of an endurance athlete. He's hiked the entire Appalachian Trail, run a half dozen Boston Marathons, climbed Mexico's three highest mountains, and, since moving to Alaska in 1984, won the 105-mile Iditashoe (a backcountry snowshoe race) eight times. But his special passion nowadays is to roam Chugach State Park.

Lyons's work commitments don't usually allow him more than a day or two away from town, but that's no problem because he's not a backpacking sort. He prefers to go light and fast and long, on extended day and overnight hikes beyond the trail system. Usually he goes solo, not because he's antisocial, but for the flexibility it offers. "I don't spend a lot of days in the park, but I do a lot of miles. One of my days is like a 2- or 3-day trip for most people," he chuckles. "Most times I'll keep hiking right through the night." His longest Chugach hike to date was a 40-hour, 80-mile off-trail marathon from the Knik River, at the park's northern tip, to Girdwood, at its southern edge. And in 1990, he climbed all 12 of the front range's 5,000-foot peaks—a journey of 45 miles and 21,000 feet in elevation gain—in 27½ hours.

A passionate ridge-walker, Lyons is drawn toward all mountains, but he's become especially attached to the Chugach Range, with its familiar moods and never-ending surprises: sudden storms, unexpected meetings with wildlife, hidden alpine lakes, dramatic shifts in the quality of light. "So many people go north to Denali or south to the Kenai Peninsula, but to me the attraction is right here," he says. "I can go from work to the mountains in a half hour; and once you get a few miles from the trailhead, you'd never know you're within a few miles of the city. It's just you and the mountains and the wildlife."

Jim Sayler and Willie Hersman are two others who've been smitten by the Chugach, though they're more fascinated by its vertical charms. Hersman, a geologist, is the only person to climb all 21 of the western Chugach's 7,000-foot peaks—including 16 within the park—while Sayler, a community school's coordinator, is one shy. In all, Hersman has ascended nearly 100 of Chugach State Park's 155 mountains; Sayler had done all but three by fall of 1995. Such commitment to the Chugach Mountains is exceptional; the range is largely overlooked by mountaineers, even those living in Anchorage. Hersman guesses that only a dozen or so locals actively climb Chugach peaks.

Part of the problem is access. Even the park's most difficult mountains can be climbed in a single day, but several require approaches of 4 to 5 days. And most climbers planning a 1- or 2-week trip will head for bigger hills. "People want something more exotic," believes Hersman, a historian for the Anchorage-based Mountaineering Club of Alaska. "If a lot of these peaks were in the Alps, they'd have established routes and be climbed regularly."

Another problem is the rock. Originally deposited as volcanics and sediments, it's been transformed by geologic forces into crumbly metamorphics known locally as "Chugach crud." Not nearly as aesthetic or safe to climb as, say, granite.

What all this makes for, says Sayler, is "the kingdom that nobody wanted." He, more than any other contemporary climber, is an exception to that rule: "I think the Chugach [climbing] experience is every bit as spectacular as any in Alaska. Many of its mountains are visually beautiful and challenging to climb. I've always been in awe of them."

More than two decades have passed since Sayler first set foot in the park. Like so many others, Flattop was the first thing he did, "on a perfect, sunny day." But he's one of the few to push farther and farther into the backcountry. A disciplined journal keeper, Sayler figures he's walked more than 8,000 miles in Chugach State Park since 1975. "It's become a way of life," he says.

At first he simply hiked and backpacked, to get a feel for the land. But in the mid-1980s Sayler began doing what he calls the "extreme stuff": first ascents and long traverses no one had tried before. "There's nothing," he says, "like topping out on a mountain where no one has ever been before."

Every summer, Sayler picks out new routes and heads off on 7- to 10-day trips, usually alone. Almost always he has the mountains and valleys to himself, and he considers solitude to be one of the park's greatest gifts: "Use of the park has gone up a lot, but there are still vast areas where you won't see a soul."

Besides being one of the park's most active explorers, Sayler for several years has acted as an unofficial guide, introducing friends to his favorite haunts. "I love

taking people to wild, crazy places they'd never imagined in Chugach," he tells me. "It's a joy just watching their reactions."

—◦∿◦—

TRAFFIC SLOWS to a standstill. Cars begin pulling over to the side of the road. Binoculars, Instamatics™, and video cameras are grabbed. And a crowd begins to gather, as both tourists and Alaskans manuever for a better view of Dall sheep feeding less than 100 feet away.

The wild, snow-white sheep pay little attention to the human spectators. Continuing to feed on grasses and willow, they sometimes wander close to the road and show no outward signs of fear, even when people approach to within 30 feet or less. It's a scene that's repeated dozens of times each summer, along one of Alaska's busiest stretches of highway.

More than 50,000 Dall sheep inhabit the state's mountain ranges, from Southcentral Alaska north to the Arctic. They're prized wildlife symbols of three national parks: Denali, Wrangell–St. Elias, and Gates of the Arctic. But nowhere are they so accessible to the public as the Windy Corner area of Chugach State Park, a half-hour's drive from downtown Anchorage.

From April through August, ewes, lambs, and young adult rams belonging to the Falls Creek band inhabit steep cliffs and grassy meadows above the Seward Highway between Mileposts 106 and 107. Peak viewing occurs in June and early July, shortly after the ewes have given birth; visible throughout the day, the sheep are usually most easily seen in early morning. As many as 50 sheep have been spotted from the highway (20 or fewer is more the norm), but only rarely are the older, full-curl rams present—they prefer backcountry solitude.

While the sheep's high visibility is a guaranteed treat for wildlife lovers, it has proved a management headache for Chugach State Park personnel. Drivers

◀ On a July evening, a hiker stands on a Bird Ridge
rocky summit above Turnagain Arm.

who slow down or stop to watch and photograph the sheep often ignore designated turnouts and park instead along the narrow highway shoulder, despite NO PARKING signs. And as crowds gather, people pay less attention to traffic patterns.

"We're worried about the 'sheep jams,'" says Chugach State Park superintendent Al Meiners. "When people see wild sheep 3 feet from the road, they just go nuts. Other senses tend to shut down, and you get people doing foolish things, like slamming on their brakes while still on the highway. It's real dangerous, because you have other drivers coming screaming around that curve at 50, 60 miles an hour, and here's a traffic jam. I went down there once to study the problem and ended up directing traffic." The state is considering an expanded parking lot, with spotting scopes, to lure drivers off the highway.

Biologists aren't sure why the sheep congregate in such large numbers along the roadway, but retired state wildlife manager Dave Harkness believes the cliffs overlooking the Seward Highway contribute to their tolerance of human traffic: "The sheep know they have an easy escape route if they need it. In a few minutes, or even seconds, they can be out of view." The band lives within an area that's off-limits to hunting, which also helps account for the sheep's "tame" behavior; lambs learn at an early age that people don't pose a threat. Yet, says Harkness, "come August and September, the sheep are vastly different creatures; they're not as accessible or visible. It's hard to say whether they equate danger with different times of the year."

Protection afforded the Falls Creek Band doesn't extend to the entire park; much of its backcountry is open to Dall sheep hunting from August to October, though special permits are required. State regulations allow Chugach sheep of any age or either sex to be killed, but here as in other sheep-hunting areas, mature rams with their massive, curling horns are especially prized by big-game hunters. Over the years, several trophy rams have been taken in the western Chugach.

While Windy Corner's sheep are guaranteed to draw a crowd, they are not the only major attraction, or even the biggest, along Chugach State Park's southern boundary, where for 25 miles three key elements intersect: the mountains, the Seward Highway, and Turnagain Arm.

"The Arm," as it's locally known, is a 40-mile-long estuary surrounded by the Chugach Mountains. Once a river valley, it was carved by glaciers into a deep fjord, then later filled by sediments. Now a shallow saltwater channel, at low tide it ressembles a network of muddy, braided rivers. Though starkly attractive, the Arm's mud-flats can be deadly. In places, its glacial muds and silts have the consistency of quicksand; unwary people have become trapped, then drowned in the incoming tide.

The Arm has lured humans for thousands of years. Its first known users were Stone Age Eskimos, whose tools archaeologists have dated at 6,000 to 9,000 years old. Much later came Russian fur traders and, in the late 1700s, English explorer Captain James Cook, who gave the Arm its name; here, Cook and crew had to "turn again" while searching for the Northwest Passage. Following Cook were more fur traders, then gold miners, homesteaders, railroad and highway builders, and, most recently, recreational users. For several decades, Turnagain Arm has been one of Anchorage's primary playgrounds, though most of the play is in spring and summer.

By early May the ice is usually gone, and both hooligan—oily, smelt-like fish—and humans are back in large numbers. On a cloudless spring day, with gentle breezes swirling down the Arm, bald eagles soar on thermals in search of hooligan. Far below, rock climbers practice techniques on roadside cuts, couples stroll along Turnagain Arm Trail, and families picnic at McHugh Creek. Two miles down the road at Beluga Point, people sit and stare at the thick gray water. Perhaps they're mesmerized by swirling, hypnotic patterns created by the incoming tide. Or they're looking for signs of the ghostly white beluga whales that often follow hooligan into the Arm. Belugas, in turn, are sometimes followed by hunting orcas. The presence

▲ A fisherman holds his catch of pink salmon, pulled from Bird Creek, a popular fishing stream that flows out of Chugach State Park into Turnagain Arm.

of either species is likely to slow, or stop, the flow of traffic, creating highway "whale jams" on a par with Windy Corner's sheep jams.

Depending on the season, people also come here to camp, fish for salmon at Bird Creek, windsurf the Arm's big waves—locals boast that Turnagain has the steadiest, most predictable winds in North America—hike alpine trails, climb ice, and watch for North America's second-largest bore tide, a wall of water up to 6 feet high traveling 10 to 15 miles per hour.

Though it comprises only a tiny slice of Chugach State Park's total area, the Turnagain Arm corridor is by far its most popular destination. In 1995, nearly three-quarters of the park's visitors spent time in or along the Arm.

⸻

ONLY 15 MILES NORTH of Windy Corner's sheep jams, while camped on a ridge above Ship Creek, Cliff Eames

once enjoyed what many would consider the ultimate wilderness experience. Shortly before midnight, as he and backpacking companion Mike Frank prepared for sleep, Eames's dog Spike began to growl. Peering out of the tent, the men saw two wolves standing side by side, less than 20 feet away.

Eames pulled Spike into the tent, then returned his attention to the wolves. Considerably larger than his 70-pound black Labrador, they had beautiful coats and appeared well fed. "They looked very healthy," he recalls. "Big and healthy."

Apparently more perplexed than alarmed, the wolves stared back for perhaps 30 seconds, then they nonchalantly turned and walked slowly away. About 75 yards off, they were joined by two other wolves, and together, the foursome howled for 30 to 45 seconds, then vanished quietly into the night. "The wolves didn't seem the least bit afraid," says Eames, an Anchorage resident since 1977 and, as issues director

55

for the Alaska Center for the Environment, a self-described park watchdog. "It was incredible—one of my most memorable experiences. To think, we were only an hour from our cars."

Other backcountry travelers have been equally touched by Chugach's wolves. An almost mystical encounter took place on Eklutna Glacier in 1978, when six men in two different parties got caught in a severe winter storm. Howling gales, heavy snow, and subzero windchill temperatures drove the men to a Mountaineering Club hut, where they stayed for several days, confined by near-zero visibility and winds strong enough to knock a person down. The men grew accustomed to the wind's shrieks and moans and roars. But at 5 A.M. on their final morning at the cabin, they were awakened by a new, more-surprising noise: howling wolves. The distant calls lasted a few moments, then abruptly ended. The idea of wolves traveling in pitch darkness during such a storm seemed so outrageous, so unbelievable, that the men thought perhaps they'd somehow imagined the howls, until the wolves spoke again. "It was eerie. The wolves were so loud, they must have been within 5 feet of the cabin," recalls former Chugach ranger and superintendent Pete Panarese. "There was this incredible surge of adrenalin, and we all piled out of the cabin for a look."

Gale-force winds still blew across the glacier, but visibility had improved considerably. As mountaineer Jim Sayler later reported: "Suddenly, out of the fog far across the glacier, several small shapes appeared. With the dull white light and the shifting clouds, the scene appeared like something out of *The Twilight Zone*, but at the same time held a bright, fabulous magic. . . . We watched as five wolves made their way across and down the glacier. As suddenly as they had appeared, they were gone."

The pack's passing was considered a good omen; if wolves were moving, perhaps the storm was breaking.

◄ The Eagle River rushes past golden birches and freshly snow-dusted mountains.

Later that day, conditions improved enough for the men to descend the glacier and leave the mountains, their spirits lifted in immeasurable ways.

⧓

MOST YEARS, OVERCAST and often drizzly weather is the summer norm in Chugach State Park, so when the sun does shine, crowds of people come out to play. Especially on weekends. On a midsummer Sunday afternoon, with the sun shining hotly, the Eagle River Nature Center's parking lot is filled to capacity.

Outside the nature center, a group of backpackers who've just completed the 26-mile Crow Pass crossing—Chugach's most popular overnight route—relax in the shade and trade tales from the trail. Other visitors stroll the nearby Rodak Nature Trail, a short loop with interpretive signs and a salmon-viewing deck. Inside the log structure, several youngsters conduct a hands-on inspection of fur, feathers, and bones in the "close-up corner," while Chugach volunteers answer visitor questions and offer advice.

About 25 road miles from downtown Anchorage, on the park's northwestern edge, the nature center is one of Chugach's primary gateways and gathering spots. Formerly a 1960s-vintage roadhouse, the building was purchased in 1980 and later remodeled and expanded. Among its chief attractions are natural history displays, Dall sheep spotting scopes, and a summer series of naturalist programs.

People constantly move in and out. Some have questions about trail conditions; others ask about camping, *Giardia*, or wildlife. "There's so much paranoia about bears," says seasonal ranger Jill Holdren. "People are constantly asking 'Are the bears out today?' or 'Any bear attacks today?' " Truth is, black bears are commonly seen along the Crow Pass Trail, but attacks by either black or grizzly bears anywhere in Chugach State Park are extremely rare. During the park's first 25 years, only two people were killed by a bear; both died in a 1995 attack, in which a grizzly was defending a moose carcass. Still, bears seem to be on the minds of many visitors, especially tourists, so at least once a year the park hosts a bear-awareness program at the nature center. Typically, it's the year's biggest draw.

By summer's end, more than 50,000 people will stop at the center, making it the single biggest attraction on Chugach's northern end. For many, it's the only Chugach experience they'll have; for others, it's the starting point for even grander park adventures.

Born at the foot of Eagle Glacier, the cold and silty river for which the nature center is named qualifies as Chugach State Park's only navigable stream and, with 30 of its 42 miles bordered by the park, it serves as a watery playground for hundreds of Anchorage-area river floaters. From the primary put-in (4½ miles below the visitor center), Eagle River's first 11 miles are popular with canoeists, kayakers, and rafters of almost all abilities. But Class I and II water then gives way to much more difficult white water. It's water that novice boaters should never attempt, but each year some try, with predictable consequences: busted boats and injured or hypothermic people. Or worse. At least a handful of people have died while floating Eagle River. Following the death of one canoeist in 1986, veteran river runner Jim Ramey warned, "Eagle River is not for beginners.

HUNTING

Sport hunting is generally allowed in the backcountry areas of Alaska's state parks, although discharge of weapons is prohibited within ¼ to ½ mile of park facilities. Some local hunting closures have been put in place. Most hunting seasons occur between late August and the end of October (regulations vary from region to region). For more information, contact each park's headquarters for specifics on seasons, bag limits, and other hunting regulations.

People hear that the rapids are Class II and think, 'No problem.' Well, it *is* a problem if you're a canoeist with no white-water experience. It's one thing in the Lower 48, where the water is warm. But up here, without a wet suit, you have about 5 or 10 minutes of functional time [in glacially fed streams like Eagle River]. Then you're basically a cork, floating out of control."

—∿∿—

LATE OCTOBER. Winter has returned to the Chugach Mountains. The afternoon sun casts a warm, golden glow on the landscape, but the warmth is an illusion; a cold, chilling wind rips down the mountainside. The wind plays games with snow that fell earlier in the week. Pick up the snow here, move it over there. Carve out bare spots while building drifts.

The same wind that reshapes the landscape bites at my face as I walk up Flattop. With summer giving way to winter, the mountain has undergone a radical personality change; Alaska's most-climbed peak is now cold and forbidding. Snow and subfreezing temperatures have chased away the crowds.

Suddenly the world goes silent, except for the wheezing of lungs, as I ascend a steep gully that momentarily shields me from the wind. Flattop's last 20 to 30 feet can be intimidating in winter. Wind-built snowdrifts accumulate at the top of the chute, creating a near-vertical dropoff. It's not bad when the footing is solid and the snowpack stable, but when the snow is crumbly or a heavy load has been freshly deposited . . . well, even Flattop can offer risks. On this day, there are no such problems. The snow is powdery but compact.

Finally, I'm on top. The wind again howls and cuts through my clothing. I retreat from the edge and Anchorage disappears from view. All that's left are the mountains. Private moments such as these are among my happiest times in Chugach State Park. It's been a good day, a good climb. Rejuvenated, I descend.

► Chugach autumn: hikers and llamas cross a snow-covered alpine meadow.

CHUGACH CHRISTMAS

▲ A bull moose rests in a snow-covered forest meadow, following the annual autumn rut. Chugach State Park is home to about 300 moose.

December 1994.
Christmas is coming: season of good cheer, season of darkness; holiday spirit, holiday blues; time of endings and fresh beginnings. My mood swings have seemed wilder than usual this winter, my 13th in Alaska, as though reflecting our Anchorage weather. Blue-sky days of inner calm, blown apart by stormy lows. Meltdowns, freeze-ups. Rapid shifts, back and forth. It's had me wondering about "the winds of change."

Wondering, too, about my own connections—to people, to nonhumans, to place. Last Christmas, among the gifts I received was a book of paintings by Frank Howell with poetry by Nancy Wood called *Spirit Walker*. One poem, "My Help Is in the Mountain," especially touched me. It begins: "My help is in the mountain / where I take myself to heal / the earthly wounds / that people give to me."

So it is with me and the Chugach Mountains: place of healing, release, rejuvenation, connection, joy. Though the thermometer outside the house reads 4°F at 2 P.M., skies are blue, the air is calm, and Rusty Point—a Chugach landmark visible from my yard—is bathed in golden light. A good day to be among the mountains, to visit Chugach State Park.

Walking along a forest trail, I welcome the cold as it presses in on my heavily clothed body, makes my wind pants stiffen and crinkle. I drink mountain air like chilled elixir, feel it swirl through my mouth, rush down my throat, cleanse my lungs. I feel it on my nose and cheeks, first as a coolness, then a tingling, a burning. It seeps through mittens and boots, lightly touching fingers and feet, and sends a wave of shivers through arms and shoulders. So nice, for a change, to simply be with the cold, appreciate it.

The only signs of wildlife are the tracks of moose, hares, and voles, until a flock of pine grosbeaks passes overhead. I count 14 of them dipping, swooping, chirping, and wonder if they're among the group that visits my feeders. Male grosbeaks are mostly red, females gray with yellow to olive green splotches on head and rump. Robin-sized birds, they're year-round residents of the Anchorage Bowl's spruce forests, yet I never noticed them until setting up some feeders last winter. Now they add pleasure to both my home life and winter walks. Perched atop spruce trees, whistling brightly, they ornament Chugach's forested hillsides with holiday cheer. How did I miss them for so long?

Chickadees, magpies, ravens, and a small swarm of redpolls—tiny, sparrow-like birds distinguished by black chin spots and red patches on their heads—also chatter among the trees. Redpolls, like grosbeaks, are new

acquaintances of mine, welcomed guests at my feeders.

My walk has now taken me into alpine tundra, where midafternoon's soft yellows subtly yield to peach, rose, then lavender as day's end approaches. Slowly, almost imperceptibly, the sunlight dims and disappears. In its wake is a fiery sunset that casts a purplish pink afterglow on the Chugach Range and prolongs day's passage into night.

Ravens, returning to their nighttime roosts, are silhouetted against the evening sky. Some fly alone, some in pairs. Others come in bunches; I count 15 ravens in one group, 22 in another. Across Cook Inlet, Mounts Redoubt and Iliamna stand dark against a blood-red sky, while below me Anchorage is a mass of shimmering lights. It's all beautiful, all connected. Mountains, sky, forest, city. Winter's cold. Grosbeaks and redpolls and ravens. Me.

▼ A lone hiker walks along a trail in Chugach State Park's Glen Alps area.

A JEWEL IS SAVED

▲ Hikers and Dall sheep watch each other on the summit of Flattop Mountain, one of the most popular visitor destinations in Anchorage's backyard wilderness.

Seated in an Anchorage restaurant, where she's been sharing memories and talking with a stranger about one of her life's great passions, Sharon Cissna pauses in her story, as though lost in thought. Then she smiles. It's a wide, glowing smile. "I think it was meant to happen," she says. "It was a moment in time when the right people and the right idea came together at exactly the right time. And so we saved a jewel."

The moment in time: 1969 to 1970. The jewel (and passion): Chugach State Park.

By all accounts, Chugach owes its being to a grass-roots movement of the sort rarely seen in Alaska, before or since. Cissna recalls, "There were a lot of good people involved, representing all sorts of interests. It was a community effort, in the truest sense." As with any movement, there were leaders. Instigators. *Provocateurs.* Among the most persistent and passionate was Cissna, now a 54-year-old mental health counselor and graphic artist, then a student and '60s-style activist. She'd come to visit Alaska in 1967 and, like so many others, she stayed. Before long she joined a mountaineering club and the Alaska Conservation Society and helped establish an Alaska chapter of the Sierra Club. "There wasn't much of an environmental community back then," she recalls. "We felt like lonely voices in the wilderness."

Small numbers were, however, balanced by deep dedication. Several activists, Cissna among them, met every Thursday to discuss Alaska conservation issues. Often they talked of the need for more federal and state parkland. In the late 1960s, Alaska still had no state parks and no Division of Parks. Among its unprotected lands were those in Anchorage's backyard wilderness: the Chugach Mountains.

Since the 1950s, hunters, horseback riders, skiers, and other recreational groups had tried to get parts of the western Chugach Range preserved as parkland, to no avail. The turning point came in 1969, when the state announced it would open Bird and Indian Valleys to commercial logging. Cissna considered the timber-harvest plans appalling. So did Art Davidson.

Davidson had hitchhiked to Alaska in 1964, a 20-year-old in search of climbing adventures. Surrounded by mountains, most of them still unnamed and unclimbed, he quickly fell in love with the land. And he too stayed. The Chugach Mountains were the first peaks he explored;

eventually they became his home. After a night at Powerline Pass, he hiked down into the spruce–hemlock forests of Indian Valley. "It was," he recalls, "like being in heaven." Now that forest was going to be logged.

"My immediate reaction was, 'We can't let them do that,'" Davidson says. "Besides being a beautiful place, Indian Valley was used by all kinds of community groups: Boy Scouts and Girl Scouts, skiers, hikers, horse riders, mountaineers."

Davidson, Cissna, and two other logging opponents, Ted Schultz and Skip Matthews, filed a lawsuit and forced the state to cancel the sale. Though satisfying, the court victory left Cissna wanting more. "We'd put so much energy into trying to block development," she says. "I was getting really tired of fighting *against* something. I wanted to fight *for* something." She didn't have to look hard for a cause: the federal government had already announced plans to give the state a half million acres adjacent to Anchorage, most of it in the Chugach Mountains. There'd be no better time to push for a park.

In August 1969, Cissna and about 20 other activists launched a campaign to establish a wilderness park, nearly 500,000 acres in size, in Anchorage's backyard. Things happened fast after that. Members of the Chugach State Park Ad Hoc Committee wrote letters, initiated petitions, gave slide shows, and held meetings all over town. Within a few months, they had won the support of nearly all of Anchorage's recreational groups, received the blessing of local politicians, and, by January 1970, had a bill introduced to the Alaska legislature.

Legislation creating Chugach State Park passed both the state senate and house in May 1970, and Governor Keith Miller signed it into law on August 6 of that year. Cissna, now known in some quarters as the "mother of Chugach State Park," continues to marvel at the speed and ease of it all. "By the time it got to the legislature, there was almost no drama," she says. "We had done our homework, recruited allies. . . . In one sense, we were very lucky; resistance began to build almost as soon as the park was a done deal. It needed to happen when it did, or that land would have gotten divided up, I'm sure of it."

During its first year, Chugach State Park had no headquarters, no permanent staff, no management plan, no enforcement, no visitor programs. "It was like 'wild frontier Alaska,'" says former State Parks director Neil Johannsen, "a playground for dirt bikes, jeeps, hunters, target shooters, activities that conflicted with other uses and park values. . . . People basically did whatever they pleased."

That began to change in September 1971, when Johannsen became Chugach's first superintendent.

Among his resources: a roll of maps, a snow machine, a worn-out station wagon, and a $20,000 annual budget. With no money to hire additional staff, Johannsen spent his first year working 12-hour days, 7 days a week.

Realizing it would be impossible to manage the park alone, he actively recruited allies, people with a stake in the park's future. He sought advice on how the park should be developed *and* protected, and, perhaps most important of all, he began to educate the public about the new park.

"Chugach State Park is a big damn deal," Johannsen says now. "It's the Alaskan dream: wild country, with tremendous opportunities for recreational use. Setting aside this park is one of the most significant things our state has ever done."

▼ This evening view shows the downtown Anchorage skyline and, behind it, the Chugach Mountains: an accessible wilderness on the edge of town.

▲ **Arctic ground squirrel**

IF YOU GO

Getting There: It's only a short drive from downtown Anchorage to the city's backyard wilderness. Several of the park's most popular trailheads can be reached from city streets, while other trails and park facilities are accessible from either the Glenn or Seward Highways. Maps showing trailhead locations are available at park headquarters and the Alaska Public Lands Information Center in downtown Anchorage. Aircraft access is restricted to Eklutna Lake and a nearby landing strip. Inside the park, travel is generally by foot in summer and skis in winter, though limited areas are open to bikes, ATVs, horses, motorboats, and snow machines. Check park regulations for details.

Weather: Summers tend to be cool, with mostly overcast skies and frequent rain, often as drizzle. Precipitation levels vary considerably within the park, with Chugach's southeast section, along Turnagain Arm, the wettest. Summer daytime temperatures are most commonly in the 50s and 60s, though balmy 80-degree days occasionally occur, as do summer snowstorms at higher elevations.

When to Go: The prime visitor season is June through September, but local residents frequent the park year-round. The best time to see wildflowers is from late June through early August (more than 50 species are found here, including geraniums, paintbrush, monkshood, bluebells, forget-me-nots, and fireweed); birding is best in May and June, berry picking in August and September.

Facilities and Services: Park headquarters are in the Potter Section House, MP 115 of the Seward Highway, while a nature center is located at the end of Eagle River Road and a ranger station is staffed at Eklutna Lake. There are three public campgrounds, at Eklutna Lake, Eagle River, and Bird Creek; all are road accessible and have picnic tables, fire pits, water, and latrines. Volunteers give naturalist programs weekly during the summer and less regularly in winter. A list of area campgrounds outside the park and companies that offer guide services and park tours is available from headquarters.

Activities: Spring through fall: hiking, backpacking, camping, fishing, wildlife and wildflower viewing and photography, picnicking, horseback riding, mountain biking, mountaineering, rock climbing, glacier travel, berry picking, hunting, windsurfing, paragliding, and boating. Winter: Ice climbing, snowmobiling, nordic and telemark skiing, snowshoeing, and mountaineering. Check with park managers for restrictions on certain activities, for example, hunting and snowmobiling.

Hiking: Nearly 30 trails, totaling more than 150 miles, crisscross the park; many have parking lots, information displays, and latrines at their trailheads. Among the most popular Chugach hikes are Flattop Mountain, Bird Ridge, Williwaw Lakes, Turnagain Arm Trail, and the Crow Pass Crossing.

For More Information: Contact Chugach State Park Headquarters, Milepost 115 Seward Highway, HC 52, Box 8999, Indian, AK 99540; (907) 345-5014. Other helpful resources include *A Naturalist's Guide to Chugach State Park*, by Jenny Zimmerman; *55 Ways to the Wilderness in Southcentral Alaska*, by Helen Nienhueser and John Wolfe, Jr.; and *Ridgelines*, a newspaper-style guide published by the park.

SHUYAK ISLAND STATE PARK

ISLAND PARADISE

A pair of sea otters play in aquamarine salt water, bobbing like corks in 2- and 3-foot swells. Gulls squawk while circling overhead, and waves driven by gusting winds crash endlessly against the rocky shoreline. Grassy meadows carpeted with fuchsia, azure, and lavender wildflowers cap sea cliffs 50 to 60 feet high. And beachcombers sunbathe under a deep blue, cloudless sky, shedding layers of clothing in the 70°F air.

The idyllic setting evokes comparisons to California's Big Sur coastline, even the South Sea islands. But the chill ocean water and views of distant snow-covered volcanic cones serve as reminders that this coastal paradise is located in the Pacific Ocean's northernmost reaches.

The simple truth is, cloudless days and warm weather are something of an illusion here, at the northern end of the Kodiak Archipelago. Yes, they happen—I've kayaked under cerulean skies, enjoyed the sun's warm caress on my bare skin, heard the references to Galapagos and Carmel—but not very often. The rule at Shuyak Island is thick overcast, rain, and 50°F or 60°F days. And that's in midsummer. The rest of the year is usually cooler, wetter, stormier. You can go weeks without seeing the sun.

If Shuyak is an island paradise, it's because this 46,000-acre land- and seascape is rich in fish and wildlife, wilderness solitude, and the protected

◀ An ocean paddler explores Neketa Bay's calm waters.
▲ Mulcahy View Cabin, one of four public-use cabins in Shuyak Island State Park.

waters favored by coastal explorers. As for sunbathing days, they're a wonderful, if rare, bonus. And thank goodness for their rarity. Shuyak's cool, wet climate and remoteness (250 miles southwest of Anchorage, it's accessible only by floatplane or boat) keep the crowds at bay and make it possible to go days without seeing another person.

It also helps, for those in search of solitude, that there are no towns on Shuyak. No place to buy groceries, fuel, or souvenirs. No roads, no airstrips, no harbors, no campgrounds. There is one wilderness lodge on the island's southern shore, but it's open only a few months each year. And except for the lodge's caretaker, no one lives on the island year-round.

It wasn't always this way. Ancient village sites suggest that Native peoples belonging to the Ocean Bay, Kachemak, and, most recently, the Koniag cultures lived on Shuyak for thousands of years. The Koniags lived in "semi-subterranean" sod houses, traveled in *baidarkas*—the first kayaks—and depended heavily on the region's sea mammals and fish for food. Oral tradition tells of a large Koniag community on Shuyak's southern end as recently as the late 1700s, but by the mid-19th century all of the island's Natives had been driven off by Russian fur traders and hunters.

Humans returned to Shuyak on a seasonal basis in the early 1900s, drawn by rich herring and salmon fisheries. A cannery built at Port Williams in 1930 stayed in business until the sixties, and commercial seiners still harvest silver salmon each August. In recent decades, though, Shuyak has been mostly a recreational retreat. Hunters come here for Sitka black-tailed deer and, less commonly, brown bear, while anglers are lured by silver salmon and halibut. Since the mid-1980s, the island has also attracted increasing numbers of sea kayakers. That small but steady growth can be linked to the 1984 birth of Shuyak Island State Park, an 11,000-acre unit on the island's northwestern side. The park's presence expanded Shuyak's visibility beyond the sparsely populated Kodiak region, and, as that happened, word of its nearly infinite

ocean-paddling possibilities spread to the mainland.

Besides boosting Shuyak's recreational profile—they even advertised the new park in *ALASKA* magazine—state officials made it easier to endure the island's often stormy weather. Four public-use cabins have been built within the park, available through a reservation system. Capable of housing up to eight people, they have many of the comforts of home: propane lights and two-burner hot plate, bunk beds, picnic table, and cooking utensils. There's even a kitchen sink, storage shed, outdoor shower stall, and outhouse. And the propane is provided. "The cabins have changed visitor-use patterns," says park ranger Kevin Murphy. "People are coming earlier in the summer and later in the fall, because they can get out of the weather."

Shuyak's recreational cabin system—the first to be established in any of Alaska's wilderness state parks—has proved to be extremely popular, but it created quite a stir in the mid-1980s. "People asked us, 'Why do you want to impact the environment like that?' But we feel that what we're doing is controlling the [human] impact," then-superintendent Ed Apperson said in 1987. "Before the cabins were built, people were chopping trees, leaving trash, and illegally harvesting the resources . . . bear, deer, otter, whatever. The area was so remote, it was difficult to control those sorts of activities. But since the cabins were built, that sort of thing has stopped. The presence of more people acts as a deterrent to illegal activities."

Beyond the cabins, development has been kept to a minimum, to enhance the park's scenic wildness. There are less than 10 miles of foot trails, no campgrounds or visitor centers, and a single ranger station.

———✧———

WHETHER IT'S A REFLECTION of the aging process, this desire for backcountry comfort, or simply a bow of respect to Shuyak's weather, three friends and I book the Mulcahy View Cabin for a week in August 1991. The idea is to use the cabin as our "base camp" and explore the island through daylong, or even half-day,

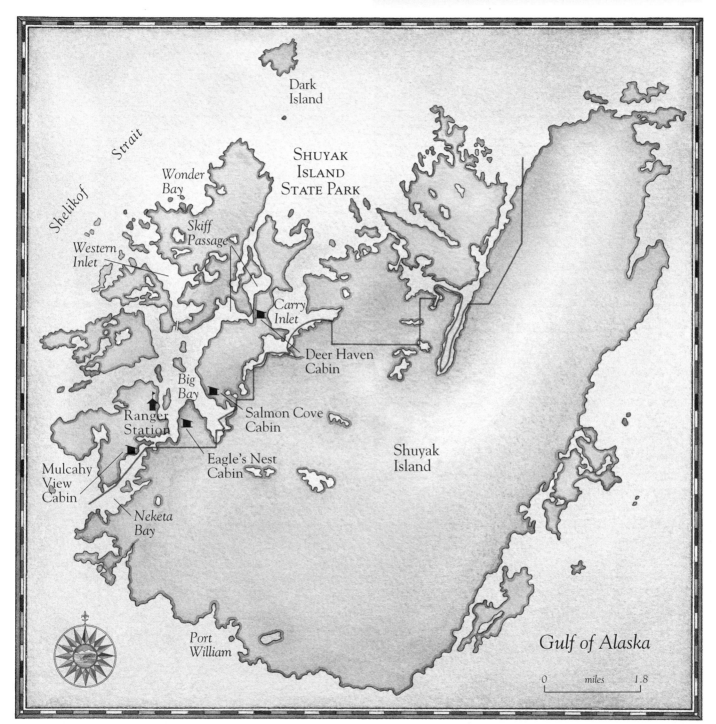

Dark
Island

SHUYAK
ISLAND
STATE PARK

Strait

Wonder
Bay

Shelikof

Skiff
Passage

Western
Inlet

Carry
Inlet

Deer Haven
Cabin

Big
Bay

Salmon Cove
Cabin

Ranger
Station

Shuyak
Island

Mulcahy
View
Cabin

Eagle's Nest
Cabin

Neketa
Bay

Port
William

Gulf of Alaska

0   miles   1.8

▲ A forest trail connects Mulcahy View Cabin with the shoreline of Neketa Bay.

southwest-facing channel that opens into Shelikof Strait and occasionally acts as a wind tunnel. Floatplane landings may be impossible here when conditions are calm at the other, more protected cabins.

Mulcahy View does have its benefits, though. Separated by a narrow isthmus from Shuyak's most popular recreational areas, Neketa Bay gets almost no motorized boat or plane traffic. So this cabin offers the best mix of comfort and quiet. And despite its relative isolation, it's the only one connected by trail to the Shuyak ranger station.

This August trip is my second to Shuyak in 4 years. Blessed with 4 days of sunshine on my previous visit, the island this time is blanketed in clouds and fog and drizzle. No matter. We tour the island's outer coastline in our double Kleppers, go for beach and forest walks, dig clams, pick blueberries from a luscious crop right outside our door, and fish for salmon. Then, when sufficiently soaked and chilled, we retreat to the cabin where we dry off, warm up by a wood-fired stove, make hot drinks, and relax in cozy comfort.

A Gulf of Alaska storm engulfs Shuyak on our last day, delaying our scheduled departure by a day and a half—nothing unusual for this time of year. We nap, read, play games, share snacks and conversation at the table, take short walks to stretch muscles, and patiently await the storm's passing. In weather like this, a cabin makes all the difference.

⟋⟍⟋⟍⟋

kayak trips. Like Shuyak's other cabins, ours was built to blend with the surrounding forest. Hidden by a canopy of old-growth spruce, the 12-by-20 structure is virtually invisible from either the air or the water, yet it's only a 5-minute walk from the shoreline.

Mulcahy View is usually the last of Shuyak's cabins to be filled, especially in late summer and fall. This is partly because it offers the poorest access to salmon streams, and most people who come here in August and September want to catch fish. But it's also because Mulcahy View overlooks Neketa Bay, a narrow

BORN OF VOLCANIC and marine sedimentary rocks, and later buried and scoured by glacial ice, Shuyak has what geologists call "subdued" topography. The island's high point is only 660 feet above the surrounding ocean, and no place within the park stands higher than 258 feet. Fourteen miles long and 11 miles across at its widest point, Shuyak is small as well as flat, the seventh-largest island in the Kodiak chain and an unnamed dot on many maps of Alaska.

More significant than its size is the fact that Shuyak sustains large stands of old-growth Sitka spruce

▲ Shuyak visitors explore the island's outer coast, which is frequently battered by coastal storms. High bluffs are covered by alpine meadows and stunted trees.

rain forest. Unlike neighboring Afognak and Kodiak, Shuyak's virgin forest has never been commercially logged, though only because a scheduled timber sale fell through in the late 1960s. This coastal rain forest is a rarity, containing only a single species of tree; elsewhere in Alaska, the spruce is mixed with hemlock and cedar. Biologists believe that Sitka spruce spread here from the mainland 800 to 1,000 years ago, either by wind, birds, floating logs, or perhaps even Natives in *baidarkas*. Now, nearly the entire island is covered by spruce, up to 200 or 300 years old. Only the island's

exposed, storm-battered outermost fringes remain bare of trees, covered instead by small, ground-hugging plants more commonly associated with alpine meadows: mosses, grasses, shrubs, wildflowers.

Shuyak's old-growth forest offers superb protection from coastal storms. "Get back into the forest, away from the shore," says Murphy, "and you can barely tell when it's storming. The forest keeps the island from getting too cold or too hot, which is why it's rich in wildlife." As many as 2,000 deer and 20 to 30 brown bears live among Shuyak's forests, as well as squirrels,

▲ A kayaker and Sitka black-tailed deer meet on Shuyak's outer coast. The island is inhabited by at least 2,000 deer.

beavers, little brown bats, ravens, eagles, and several songbird species.

Yet Shuyak's coastal and marine environment offer even greater wildlife riches. Of more than 100 bird species identified at the northern end of the Kodiak chain, the large majority are shorebirds and seabirds. Avian activity peaks in June, when migratory species pass through the region and summertime residents begin to nest. Among the high-profile species are tufted and horned puffins, black oystercatchers, gulls, cor-

morants, common and red-throated loons, marbled murrelets, mergansers, harlequin ducks, and sandpipers.

Especially appealing to most coastal explorers is the abundance of marine mammals in Shuyak's waters. Sea otters are the most commonly seen, sometimes in pods of 50 to 100 animals. But seals, sea lions, porpoises, and minke, fin, killer, gray, and humpback whales are also seasonally present. "We've witnessed lots of whale activity, especially off the northern end of the island," Murphy tells me. "There have been pods with as many as 12 to 15 humpback whales." They are thought to be summer residents, drawn by food-rich coastal waters.

The abundance of diverse marine life, combined with ruggedly picturesque coastline and views of the mountain ranges across Shelikof Strait, makes Shuyak's outer coast a kayaker's paradise, at least when seas are calm and skies clear. In stormy weather, the strait is a place to be avoided. Hurricane-force winds, monsoon-like rains, and 20- to 30-foot seas can quickly turn its waters into a death trap. Yet even when storms are stirring up Shelikof Strait, plenty of kayaking opportunities exist, thanks to the island's intricate network of protected bays, passages, and lagoons (carved by the same Ice Age glaciers that buried the island more than 10,000 years ago). Within Shuyak State Park, says Murphy, there are more sheltered waterways than anywhere else in the Kodiak chain.

The system's centerpiece is Big Bay, a five-pronged, starfish-like body of water in the heart of the park. When the weather is calm, the bay resembles a forest-lined lake. Even when storms are brewing along the outer coast, Big Bay's innermost waters are usually gentle enough for travel. None of its arms is more than 2½ miles long or 1 mile wide, but with dozens of tiny coves and lagoons to visit, it offers a bounty of hideaways.

Even greater seclusion is possible along the park's other major aquatic avenues: Neketa Bay, Western and Carry Inlets, and Skiff Passage. In those four waterways, kayakers will only rarely encounter other parties. Yet each of the four is connected with Big Bay or accessible via portages that range from 50 feet to 1½ miles. To improve access, park staff and volunteers have built portage trails that connect Big Bay to Western and Carry Inlets.

Shuyak's protected inner waters are ideal for novice kayakers, which is what I was in July 1987, when I first visited the island. Largely ignorant about both Shuyak and ocean paddling, I'd been enticed here by Sam Barber and Paul Ellis, co-owners of an adventure-travel company. Sam and Paul hoped to establish a kayak tour

business in the park, and I was one of three guinea pigs they recruited for a 5-day trial run; Mary and John were the others.

—◁◊▷—

A HALF HOUR NORTH of Kodiak, our bush pilot delivers us to Big Bay and Salmon Cove Cabin. After a quick lunch, Sam gives me an equally quick kayaking lesson—everyone else is an experienced paddler—then we take a short, get-acquainted tour of Big Bay.

Sam cajoles us into a prebreakfast paddle the next morning, despite continued fog and drizzle. In the gray, early morning light we spot a dozen Sitka black-tailed deer feeding on shrubs along the shore. Native to the rain forests of Southeast Alaska and British Columbia, these small deer—adult males average about 120 pounds—were first introduced to the Kodiak chain in the 1920s, as part of the territorial legislature's game-transplant program. The primary intention was to improve hunting opportunities for local hunters (brown bears are the chain's only indigenous big-game species). No deer were put on Shuyak itself, but biologists guess they spread here by swimming over from neighboring Afognak.

Dipping our paddles gently into Big Bay's glassy waters, we approach slowly and silently to within 30 feet of the deer. They're dressed in their summer coats of reddish brown; come winter, their fur will change to a darker gray-brown. The deer lift their heads to watch but seem more curious than unnerved by our presence. Once we've passed, they lower their heads and resume eating.

By noon the fog has burned off to reveal deep blue skies, the start of 4 days of sunshine and 60°F to 70°F temperatures. There's a soft breeze, but only a slight chop on the water, so we paddle out Neketa Bay to Shelikof Strait, the 20- to 25-mile-wide expanse of open water that separates the Kodiak Archipelago from mainland Alaska. Along the way we see several more deer, and for a few minutes we are escorted by a pair of cavorting sea otters that seem as curious about us as we are about them. And all around us—in the water, overhead, and along the shore—are birds. Among the most

73

eye-catching are black oystercatchers, strange-looking crow-sized shorebirds with long red bills, pink legs, yellowish eyes, and all-black bodies. Oystercatcher bills have a specialized, chisel-like tip, which enables them to be an efficient predator of mussels, clams, and barnacles. Their call is a loud whistle: *whee-whee-whee-whee*.

Our group splits up the next day, Paul and I choosing to fish rather than paddle into 30-mile-per-hour winds. We catch 20 or more Dolly Varden, keeping a handful for dinner, and Paul also lands our first and only pink salmon. Our third morning, despite continued (but diminished) winds, we rejoin Sam and the others for another day trip to the outer coast. After an hour of hard paddling, we take shelter on a protected gravel beach. Out of the wind, it's warm enough for sunbathing. "Can this be Alaska?" marvels Mary. "Maybe we got blown off course."

Upon reaching the outer coast, we again beach our kayaks and scramble to the top of volcanic bluffs. A game trail follows the cliff line, and along its edges are the bleached bones of deer, a patch of feathers, and sea urchin fragments. This seems to be a popular place for bears, otters, and shorebirds to feed. Perhaps, in previous centuries, it was also popular with Shuyak's first people. Beneath the cliffs and beyond the breaking surf, sea otters dive for fish, sea urchins, crabs. And out past the otters, aquamarine water stretches to the horizon, where it meets azure blue sky. The only clouds are across the strait, hanging over mainland mountains.

—◦◦◦—

THERE ARE PLACES (like people) that take hold of a person's psyche, refuse to let go. They stay with us, even when separated by great distances, find a place in our hearts. And inevitably they lure us back. Shuyak is such a place for me. One, two, three years pass, but I know I'll return. And I do, in 1991.

I come with different people, good friends with whom I wish to share the island. We stay in a different cabin, in a different season. And the weather couldn't be more different. Wet, foggy, stormy. The island is not so much glorious as moody. Seductive. This trip I spend less time along the outer coast, more time in the company of the forest and the quiet beaches and dark waters of Neketa Bay. We see no deer or bears but are privileged to watch two humpback whales pass by. Several miles off the island, they send their huge bodies hurtling out of Shelikof Strait's steel gray waters, then crash back down. Again and again they breach, two dozen times before I lose track. A fleeting connection between starkly dissimilar worlds. The same day we watch whales, we're escorted by Dall porpoises. Smaller and more streamlined than whales, these black-and-white cetaceans seem well suited to their out-of-water sailing. The porpoises parallel our kayaks for a few hundred yards, then suddenly vanish.

Not as spectacular, but nevertheless delightful, are the other marine creatures of Neketa Bay: snorting, squealing river otters, which routinely approach us as we paddle, then dive and disappear, as though their curiosity's been satisfied; harbor seals silently patrolling the bay in ones or twos with just their heads poking above the water; and thousands of glutinous, tentacled jellyfish that float in and out of the bay with the tides. Most are transparent, nickel- and dime-sized, but others reach the size of a dinner plate, and a few have thick orange-brown insides and streaming tentacles that stretch 20, 30 feet.

Not a day passes without at least a short paddling voyage along Neketa's convoluted shoreline. And twice we portage our kayaks across the isthmus into Big Bay, to go fishing for silvers. The salmon are late, we're told, but dozens of flashing, ocean-bright silvers jump wildly about our kayaks. I fish until one is caught for dinner.

Paddling among schools of salmon, listening to gulls, and thinking of forests and deer, whales and otters, I am struck again by the island's abundance. And I recall what another Shuyak visitor once said: that it would be difficult to starve here. Such richness of life is what kept the Koniag people here for generations, and it's a big part of what will bring me back again. That, and Shuyak's coastal solitude.

AIR TRAVEL

▲ A floatplane glides across glassy smooth waters, as Homer bush pilot Bill DeCreeft arrives to pick up visitors who've been staying at a Shuyak cabin.

With most of the state easily accessible only by air, it should come as no surprise that Alaska is the "flyingest" state in the U.S., with roughly 1 in every 60 residents (nearly 9,500 people) a pilot—about six times the national average.

But you don't have to be a pilot yourself to reach remote corners of Alaska. Every region of the state is served by air-taxi operators, who routinely transport travelers and their gear into backcountry wilderness areas via wheeled airplanes or floatplanes.

To be sure of getting a seat, reserve charter flights well in advance of your trip. Costs vary widely, depending on party size, destination, amount of gear, and type of plane you travel on. Most air-taxi operators have standard charter rates (usually based on flight time) for the more popular destinations. Pickup locations and times are arranged in advance, but wilderness visitors should anticipate delays; the safest pilots don't fly in marginal weather. Lists of air-taxi services permitted to fly in the different state parklands can be obtained from each park's headquarters.

75

OF HUMANS AND BEARS

▲ A female brown bear and her cubs stand on their hind legs to get a better view. Brown bear moms are extremely protective of their young.

I used to have nightmares about bears. They entered my dreamworld in the mid-1970s, shortly after I came to Alaska, and they roamed the forests of my subconscious for many years after. A geologist then, just out of graduate school, I spent my first Alaskan summers in some of the state's wildest, most remote grizzly bear country. And each summer, usually toward the end of the field season,

phantom grizzlies would stalk me, chase me, attack me. They lurked in my dream shadows, ominous and haunting. I now sometimes wonder if those nightmares were omens. Perhaps they spoke of things to come, of a July afternoon in 1987, in Shuyak Island State Park.

Five of us have spent the morning in kayaks; now it's time to stretch muscles and explore one of the many

76

small islands that border Shuyak's northern coast. The islet we choose is inhabited by Sitka black-tailed deer; from the water, we see several animals feeding in open meadows. It's also home to a brown bear female, with three tiny cubs. We'd spotted them earlier in the day, though the bear family has since disappeared into the forest.

I've seen many grizzlies, but this was my first sighting of brown bears, the coastal cousins of griz. Alaska's brown bears tend to be more chocolaty in color and have smaller humps and shorter claws than their Interior relatives. On the average, they're much larger animals, mainly because they have access to more-plentiful, energy-rich foods, especially salmon. A large male grizzly may weigh 600 to 700 pounds in fall, when it's fattened for hibernation. But the largest brown bears are twice that size. And nowhere do brown bears grow larger than on the Kodiak Archipelago, home to the subspecies *Ursus arctos middendorffi*. Even here, researchers say, adult females only rarely reach 700 pounds, though this mother bear appeared much bigger.

We beach our kayaks, then split up. I go with Sam, one of the expedition's guides, following a game trail that begins in meadow but soon borders a thick stand of spruce. Sam calls out to announce our presence: "*Hooyah . . . hooyah.*"

Eventually the trail peters out, where the forest reaches the island's edge. We have a simple choice: return down the trail or cut through the woods. Sam chooses the trees and I follow, despite some misgivings. He's the guide, after all.

The spruce are 20 to 30 feet high, spindly, and densely packed, and we can't easily see more than 10 to 15 feet ahead, sometimes less. We're walking slowly, talking loudly, when suddenly my worst nightmare comes true: a bear charges out of the forest's shadows. She must have tried to hide her family in this stand to avoid the strange two-legged invaders of her island. But

we've entered her sanctuary and threatened, however innocently, her offspring. Retreat hasn't worked, so her only option now is to defend her cubs by force.

Things begin to speed up and, simultaneously, move in slow motion around me. Less than 20 feet away, the bear is a blur of terrible speed, size, and power—a dark image of unstoppable rage. Her face is indistinct, and I sense, more than see, her teeth and claws. Two giant bounds are all it takes for the bear to reach Sam, 5 feet in front of me. Somewhere, amid the roaring that fills my head, I hear a cry: "*Oh, no.*" I'm certain that Sam is about to die or be seriously mauled, and fear that I may be also.

The last thing I see is the bear engulfing Sam. Then, despite everything I've learned about bears, I turn and run, breaking one of the cardinal rules of bear encounters. But my instincts are strong, and they tell me to get out of sight, out of the woods. Climbing one of these slender trees isn't an option, and without any weapon there's nothing I can do to help Sam. The only question now is whether the bear will come after me when it's done with him. I run out of the forest onto a narrow stretch of beach; I must find the other three members of the party, get Sam's rifle from his kayak, and try to rescue him.

Back in the forest, Sam is doing what he must to survive. As the bear charges, Sam tells us later, he ducks his head and falls backward. Falling, he sees the bear's open mouth, its teeth and claws. Hitting the ground, he curls into a fetal position, to protect his head and vital organs, and offers the bear a shoulder to chew on instead. And with the bear breathing in his face, he plays dead.

The bear grabs Sam in a "hug," woofs at him, and bats him a few times like a kitten playing with a mouse. But she strikes him with her paws, not her claws. There's no sound of tearing flesh. And when, after several moments—or is it minutes?—there's no reponse from her victim, the bear ends her attack just as suddenly as she began it. The threat removed, she leaves with her cubs.

I'm still standing on the beach, listening and looking for any sign of the bear, when, incredibly, I hear Sam shout: "The bear's gone. . . . I'm all right." Miraculously, he's uninjured, except for a small scratch on the back of his hand, which he got when he fell backward into a small spruce. For someone who's just been attacked by a bear, Sam is taking the incident much more calmly than I. Perhaps, I'll learn later, this is because he's had lots of experience in such matters. He'd been "false charged" by bears three times previously.

Sam quickly recounts his story, then says, "Thank goodness it was a friendly bear. It wasn't looking for a fight; it was trying to make a point: 'Leave me alone.' " Hours later, when we're rehashing the attack, he adds: "I felt no sense of aggression or panic. I believe animals can sense a person's energy. If you're projecting aggression, or if the adrenaline is flowing, they know it. I was very calculating as to what I should do." It turns out he did everything right—once the bear attacked. Listening to Sam's story, still pumped with adrenaline, I can only shake my head and marvel at our escape.

Heading across a meadow to warn the others, we see the sow 100 yards away, still greatly agitated. She stands up, then falls back to all fours and runs around in circles, and stands up again. She's looking down the island, and we guess that she's seen or smelled our companions. The bear stands one final time, then turns sharply and lopes into another, larger spruce stand. She's followed by her cubs, three teddy bear–sized creatures. Strung out in a line, they run hard to keep up with mom.

We rendezvous with the others, quickly retell our story, and leave the bears' island. Back in camp, we talk for hours about the encounter and second-guess ourselves. We agree it was foolish to visit the island, given our earlier bear sighting, and even more foolhardy to cut

through the woods. I'm reminded, again, to question authority and trust my own judgment.

The encounter also raises questions about firearms, which may be carried in all of Alaska's state parks. I've never carried a gun into Alaska's backcountry; I'm not a firearms expert, have no desire to be, and believe that guns cause more trouble than bears. Like Sam, I also believe that guns change a person's "energy," change the way a person relates to wild places, wild creatures. They offer security, but they also can prompt people to take chances they ordinarily wouldn't, sometimes resulting in confrontations that might have been avoided. The usual result is injury or death, most often for the bear.

For a while, after the Shuyak attack, I questioned my philosophy. It's often said that bears, like people, are individuals. Each one is different, unpredictable. As Richard Nelson, an Alaskan writer, anthropologist, and naturalist whose philosophy I greatly respect, says in *The Island Within:* "All it takes is once in a lifetime, the wrong bear in the wrong place. Without a rifle (and the knowledge of when and how to use it), the rest of the story would be entirely up to the bear. . . . It's my way of self-preservation, as the hawk has its talons, the heron its piercing beak, the bear its claws. . . ." But as time has passed, I've become more convinced than ever that it's right, for me, to walk unarmed in Alaska's backcountry. It would be different, perhaps, if brown or black bears preyed on people. But they rarely do. In a sense, my choice is a symbolic gesture of respect to the animal and its world; I'm only a visitor in the bear's realm, passing through and intending no harm.

On Shuyak, we provoked the attack. A mother was being crowded, and she wanted to eliminate what she perceived as a very real threat. She was protecting her cubs, no more, no less. Playing dead, removing the threat, proved the best thing to do, not fight back. Shooting her would have been a tragedy.

SOME TIPS ON
BEARS

Though most bears avoid people whenever possible, wilderness travelers should take the following steps to minimize chance encounters with bears:

- Most attacks occur when a bear is surprised or feels threatened, so avoid sudden encounters. Whenever possible, travel in groups in open country during daylight hours and make noise when passing through forested areas or thick brush.
- Keep alert and look for signs of bears, such as fresh tracks, bear scat, matted vegetation, and partly consumed salmon. Leave the family dog at home; dogs can provoke encounters.
- When camping, pitch your tent well away from trails, streams with spawning salmon, and berry patches. Avoid areas where scavengers have gathered or that have a rotten smell; bears will often aggressively defend their food supplies.
- Cook meals at least 100 feet from tents and store food away from campsites, hung high between trees, whenever possible. If you've been fishing, change your clothes before entering your tent and store them away from camp. Avoid odoriferous foods and wash up after cooking and eating. Store garbage in an airtight container or burn it, and pack out the remains.

- If you encounter a bear, talk to it but don't yell. Don't run; running from a bear is usually the worst possible action because it will trigger a bear's predatory instincts (and bears can easily outrun humans). Back away slowly, and give the bear an escape route.
- As a rule, bigger is better with bears. If there's some way to increase your size, do it; raise your arms above your head. With two or more people, it helps to stand side by side. In a forested area, it might be appropriate to climb a tree. But remember: black bears and young grizzlies can climb.
- If a bear charges and makes contact, fall to the ground and play dead. Lie flat on your stomach or curl into a ball, hands behind your neck, and remain passive. Once a bear feels there is no longer a threat, the attack will usually end. The one exception to this rule is when a bear shows predatory behavior. Instead of charging, a hunting bear will show intense interest while approaching at a walk or a run, or by circling. If you're certain that you're being treated as prey, fight back. Such circumstances are exceedingly rare and most often involve black bears.
- Only carry a gun if you know how to use it. One possible alternative is red-pepper spray, which comes in aerosol cans. Because the canisters sometimes leak, it's best to store bear sprays in airtight containers. Notify pilots that you are carrying bear sprays when flying into backcountry areas; a leak could disable a pilot and lead to a crash.
- A summary of bear-safety tips is available in a free brochure titled *Bear Facts*, published jointly by several state and federal agencies in Alaska. Another excellent resource is Stephen Herrero's book *Bear Attacks: Their Causes and Avoidance*.

STATE PARK REGULATIONS AND FEES

These regulations and guidelines apply to all Alaska state parks:

- Reservations are not required for any facilities, except rental cabins.
- Permits are required for large groups and commercial activities.
- Pets must be kept on a leash at developed facilities, such as campgrounds, and under control in other areas at all times.
- Motor vehicles are generally restricted to roads and parking lots. For information on areas open to off-road vehicles, contact the appropriate park office.
- All litter and trash must be removed or placed in trash cans, if available. When traveling in the backcountry, pack out what you pack in, including used toilet paper.
- Horseback riding is allowed in designated areas.
- Discharge of firearms is prohibited within ¼ to ½ mile of developed facilities. No target practice is allowed.
- Fishing and hunting regulations can be obtained from the Alaska Department of Fish and Game. Information can also be obtained from park offices.
- Fires must be confined to designated sites. Portable stoves should be used in the backcountry.
- Fireworks and explosives are prohibited.
- Wildflower picking and stripping bark from trees are prohibited.
- Removal or disturbance of any cultural artifacts is prohibited.
- Aircraft landings are restricted in some parks; check for regulations at local park offices.
- Alaska's state park campgrounds, boat launches, public-use cabins, and some parking areas require user fees. For information, contact the Alaska Department of Natural Resources Information Center, 3601 C Street, Suite 200, Anchorage, AK 99503-5929; (907) 269-8400.

◄ Fishing for salmon, Skuyak Island State Park

▲ **Alaskan brown bear**

IF YOU GO

Getting There: Located at the northern end of the Kodiak Archipelago, 250 miles southwest of Anchorage, Shuyak Island can be reached by either floatplane or boat, usually from either Kodiak or Homer. A list of air-charter services that fly to the island is available from the Division of State Parks. Once at Shuyak, travel is easiest by boat; the park has no roads and few trails. Folding kayaks can be transported to the island by plane, then used to explore the park's interconnected system of bays, inlets, and passages. The Division of State Parks has published a pamphlet that describes five sea kayaking day trips within the park.

Weather: Shuyak's summers are generally cool and wet, with temperatures in the 40°F to 60°F range. The island, however, is subject to severe and unpredictable weather that often changes quickly, with little or no warning. Flights into the island are often delayed by stormy weather; visitors should therefore bring extra food and fuel.

When to Go: June through August is best, though deer hunters use the island into winter. June is a prime time for wildlife viewing, while July usually has the best weather and marks the peak of the wildflower bloom. August is the busiest month, largely because of Shuyak's silver salmon runs.

Facilities and Services: Shuyak has four recreational cabins, available on a first-come, first-served basis by reservation, no more than 180 days in advance. The 12-by-20-foot cabins are equipped with a two-burner hot plate and lights (bottled propane supplied), cooking utensils, stainless steel sink, woodstove, firewood, four full-sized bunks with pads, picnic table with benches, manual (outdoor) shower and wash area, latrine, wood and game storage shed, and "cooling box." The maximum stay is 7 days per cabin, per month; daily costs vary with the season and party size; contact the Alaska State Parks System for specifics. There are no campgrounds, but backcountry camping is allowed throughout the park. Between late May and mid-October, a ranger cabin on Big Bay is staffed with park personnel.

Activities: Sea kayaking, camping, hiking, wildlife viewing and photography, fishing, and hunting.

Hiking: Only a few short trails presently exist, though there are plans to expand the trail system. A forest trail connects Mulcahy View Cabin with the ranger station, and easy, scenic off-trail hiking is possible along tundra-covered bluffs that overlook Shelikof Strait.

For More Information: Contact Alaska State Parks, S.R. Box 3800, Kodiak, AK, 99615; (907) 486-6339. Shuyak's public-use cabins can be reserved either through the Kodiak office or through State Parks System headquarters, 3601 C Street, Suite 200, P.O. Box 107001, Anchorage, AK, 99510-7001; (907) 269-8400.

▼ **Wild iris**

81

DENALI

DENALI STATE PARK

IN THE SHADOW OF THE HIGH ONE

There it is, that big thing in the middle."

"Show me again. Where is it?"

"Where's what?"

"Mount McKinley. It's disappeared behind the clouds right now, but we could see its summit clearly just a few minutes ago."

So the conversation goes at Milepost 135.2 of the George Parks Highway, on a partly overcast June day. There's enough blue sky to raise people's hopes of seeing McKinley and enough cloud cover to mostly hide the mountain also commonly known by its Athabascan name: *Denali,* The High One.

Only 42 miles from the highway turnout, North America's highest peak rises 20,320 feet above sea level. Even more staggering, it looms 18,000 feet above the surrounding tundra and river valleys, a greater vertical rise than any other mountain on earth. Denali's height, combined with its subarctic location, makes it one of the coldest mountains on earth, if not *the* coldest. Even in June, nighttime temperatures on its upper slopes may reach -40°F. Denali is so massive that it creates its own weather systems, occasionally producing storms with winds above 150 miles per hour. The mountain is also frequently battered by storms born in the North Pacific; and because of its northerly location, scientists estimate the available oxygen on Denali's summit is equal to that of Himalayan peaks 2,000 to 3,000 feet higher. For all

◄ A backpacker rests on Kesugi Ridge; across the valley, Denali rises above its neighbors.

▲ A skier explores the Peters Hills. In the distance is 20,320-foot Denali.

▲ A signpost on Kesugi Ridge offers trail information.

these reasons, Alaska's "great ice mountain" has earned a reputation as the ultimate challenge in North American mountaineering.

Yet for every person who attempts to climb Denali—about a thousand a year—hundreds more appreciate its grandeur from afar. All that most visitors want is to see the giant granite monolith; one good look and maybe a few pictures are enough. But even that can be a challenge. Most years, it's clearly visible only 1 in 3 days from Memorial Day through Labor Day, the prime tourist season. Visitors on tight schedules, as many are, can't afford to be picky. If Denali comes out, it makes sense to stop at the nearest pullout and catch a glimpse. Though it's best known as the centerpiece of Denali National Park and Preserve, the mountain is often more easily seen from the Parks Highway, the principal road linking Anchorage and Fairbanks. And among the highway's most popular Denali viewpoints is the paved turnout at Milepost 135.2, a convenient, scenic rest stop in Denali State Park, "Little Denali."

Back in late 1960s, some visionary Alaskans imagined a state park that would capitalize on both the new Parks Highway (completed in 1972) and Denali's tremendous tourist appeal. Less than a 3-hour drive from Anchorage, this park would relieve some of the growing visitor pressure at what was then McKinley National Park. More important to state interests, it would become a major year-round destination, complete with luxurious hotel, visitor center, snowmobile trails, and scenic ridgetop drive.

All of the grandiose schemes promoted in the late 1960s and later years have so far failed. Among the most accessible of all Alaskan parklands—it's bisected by the Parks Highway and bordered on its eastern edge by the Alaska Railroad—325,460-acre Denali State Park remains one of the least known. What politicians have been unable to do, however, the tourism industry may soon accomplish. Princess Tours is building an $18 million lodge along the Parks Highway, on private land just inside Denali State Park's border. Scheduled to open in 1997, the newest Princess Hotel will inevitably make the park more of a destination.

Leaving the roadside crowd of Denali viewers, I travel north 12 miles to Byers Lake Campground. Less than half its campsites are taken at midday, and I leisurely drive through spruce–birch forest to find one that appeals. Like most highway travelers, I hurried past Byers Lake for years. Then, one September, after a particularly hectic visit to "Big Denali," I stopped on my return to Anchorage and found bliss: numerous vacant campsites—and no clouds of dust, crowds, RV caravans, or rush of people. Instead, a rich autumnal serenity. Birch leaves floated softly from trees to earth, the sweet-sour fragrance of ripening high-bush cranberries filled the air, and somewhere out on the nearby lake, a loon wailed loudly in its haunting, mournful way.

Now, in June, leaves are opening, not falling, and the cranberries that survived winter have lost their pungency. But the campground is again subdued. The only sounds are the gentle swish of wind through needles and leaves, the occasional chatter of red squirrels, and the whistles and chirps of chickadees, warblers, and thrushes. Out on Byers Lake, two anglers sit in a raft,

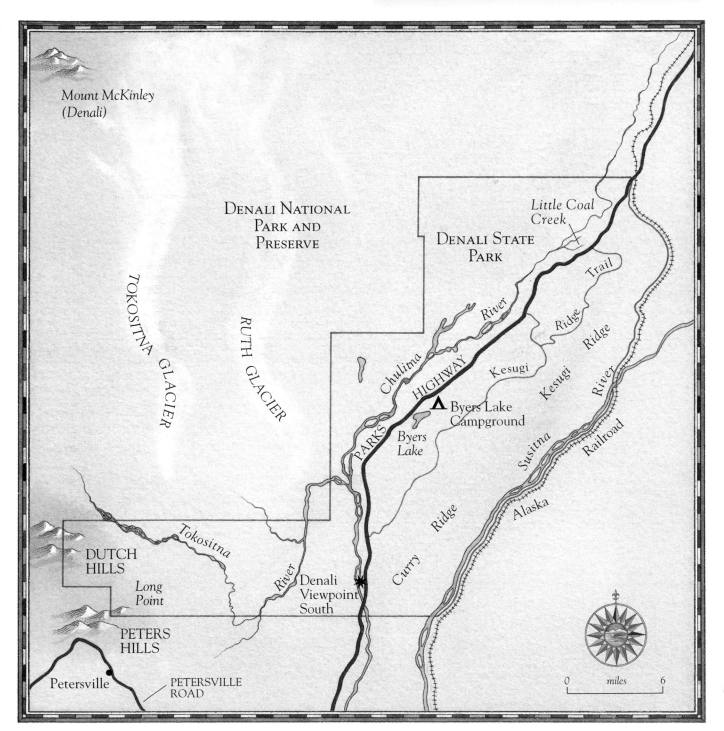

Mount McKinley
(Denali)

DENALI NATIONAL
PARK AND
PRESERVE

DENALI STATE
PARK

Little Coal
Creek

TOKOSITNA GLACIER

RUTH GLACIER

Chulitna

River

HIGHWAY

Trail

Ridge

Kesugi

Ridge

Kesugi

River

Byers Lake
Campground

PARKS

Byers
Lake

Susitna

Railroad

Alaska

Curry

Ridge

Tokositna

DUTCH
HILLS

River

Denali
Viewpoint
South

Long
Point

PETERS
HILLS

Petersville

PETERSVILLE
ROAD

0   miles   6

▲ Backpackers follow a primitive trail across Kesugi Ridge. Kesugi and neighboring Curry Ridge form the backbone of Denali State Park.

waiting patiently for a fish to bite, while on shore a family of four picnics beside the lake, an older couple walks arm-in-arm through the campground, and two bearded backpackers enter the forest. And the rest of the highway's travelers keep passing by.

⁓⁓⁓

FOURTH OF JULY WEEKEND. After too many summers of saying "next year," I'm camped on Kesugi Ridge. My day began 9 hours ago in Anchorage, under dark, drizzly skies. Now, at 3:30 P.M., I lounge beside a mountain pond, beneath brilliant heavens. But the promise of sunshine and 70-degree warmth isn't what drew me here; it could just as easily be foggy or raining. I've come to loll on luscious moss carpets, nap among purple monkshood and fuchsia shooting stars, and walk in the footsteps of grizzlies and black bears. I'm here to watch eagles ride thermals until they become black dots

on an infinite blue canvas and to follow rocky ridges wherever they take me. But mostly I'm here because I'm curious about this place called Kesugi Ridge.

Built from a mixture of volcanics, sediments, and granite, Kesugi is a 4- to 6-mile-wide, northeast-trending spine of rock that parallels the Parks Highway for 25 miles. The ridge lies just east of the highway and is easy to spot, but most road-bound travelers overlook it because eyes are inevitably drawn to the west, where Denali and its satellite peaks leap into the sky.

Quite ordinary in comparison, Kesugi and neighboring Curry Ridge barely edge past 4,500 feet, and instead of jagged spires or enormous rock walls, the tundra-topped ridges have a gently rolling nature. Considered the upland "backbone" of Denali State Park, they're more plateau than mountain.

Kesugi—a Tanaina Indian word meaning "The Ancient One"—is nonetheless considered among

Southcentral Alaska's premier backpacking routes. One reason is the view. The Alaska Range, a remote mountain kingdom of knife-edged ridges and granite walls larger than Yosemite's, dominates the western horizon. And rising above it all, the snow- and ice-capped throne of Denali. Many of the same great peaks can be seen from the highway, but the ridgetop shows the full panoramic sweep of mountains, glaciers, tundra-covered foothills, wooded lowlands, and glacial rivers.

Kesugi also offers hikers and backpackers easy access to pristine alpine backcountry less than 5 miles from the highway. All it takes is a few hours of uphill grunt work, thanks to a 36-mile trail network pioneered in the mid-1970s by state park ranger Dave Johnston and Young Conservation Corps members. The best place to get above treeline quickly is Little Coal Creek, where it's only 1½ miles and 715 feet of vertical gain from trailhead to tundra. It's at this trailhead that I've joined seven other backpackers on a 3-day, 16.7-mile holiday "tour" of Kesugi Ridge.

We start out among spruce and birch trees, chased by mosquitoes and serenaded by thrushes. From the forest we emerge into the subalpine zone, where a series of switchbacks takes us past alders, willows, geraniums, bluebells, and cow parsnips. Then, finally, alpine tundra. Above treeline, the hiking is ideal. The dirt path we follow is narrow and occasionally disappears, but the route is well marked by rock cairns. It would be difficult to get lost here, though not impossible when fog or low clouds roll in.

After setting up camp beside a tundra pond, I climb a gentle ridge above our lake and sit among volcanic boulders that have grown thick lichen beards. Far below, the Parks Highway is a narrow gray ribbon winding through lowland forests and paralleling the glacially fed Chulitna River. I scan the landscape with binoculars, but find no other signs of human development. It's hard to imagine that government bureaucrats once planned to build a scenic road and 300-room hotel along this ridge. Nothing got built, but that '60s tourism scheme led, in a roundabout way, to Denali

State Park's birth 2 years later. The developers' dream didn't die, though. In 1989, state parks officials again proposed a visitor center and lodge complex for Kesugi's northern flanks. The plan sparked a lawsuit, filed by several individuals and conservation groups, and it eventually died in court.

Below me, another group of backpackers is crossing the tundra, and two new tents have sprouted on the grassy bench. Wishing to be alone with Kesugi a while longer, I climb higher, to the ridge's eastern edge. Several thousand feet below is the Susitna River, one of the region's largest glacial streams. Beyond it are green rolling hills and broad forested plateaus that seem to stretch forever. Dark clouds drop scattered showers on distant hills, and returning to camp I wonder how long our good luck with the weather will last.

Not long, it turns out. By morning, Kesugi Ridge is also in the clouds, and where the Alaska Range stood yesterday, there's only a flat wall of gray. The day becomes a blur of fog and clouds, of rolling tundra and creek crossings. We see lots of wildflowers and birds, a red fox and ground squirrels. No bears, but lots of grizzly conversation, inspired by bear scat and holes where they've been digging. Kesugi's Troublesome Creek Trailhead is routinely closed from mid-July through September 1 because of the potential for bear-human conflicts, and a few years earlier, on an end-to-end Kesugi trip, a friend saw nine black bears in 4 days.

At 5:30 P.M. we reach our campsite, a grassy meadow beside a sparkling clear and deliciously cold mountain brook. We've only traversed a third of the ridge route, but tomorrow we'll be leaving Kesugi. The others retire to their tents early, but I stay out among the tundra flowers and songbirds. At 10 P.M., the sky opens just enough for one short burst of intense orange light, and the landscape takes on a surrealistic glow. A parting gift from The Ancient One.

—◦◦◦—

LABOR DAY WEEKEND. Summer's end, and another backpacking trip into Denali State Park's alpine

▲ Late evening light falls on tents and alpine tundra during a Fourth of July visit to Kesugi Ridge, in Denali State Park.

backcountry. This time I'm alone, camped at 3,400 feet on a gentle ridge in the Peters Hills, sixteen miles west of the Parks Highway and five miles south of Big Denali. If, looking at a map, you imagine the park to be an oddly shaped, west-facing boot, I'm next to the boot's toes. Five miles from the nearest road, I'm also a mile away from Long Point, where, it is said, Alaskan landscape artist Sydney Laurence gained much of the inspiration for his famous paintings of Denali. Both the man and the mountain have, in a sense, led me here.

The Peters Hills, I've been told, offer even more fantastic views of Denali than Kesugi Ridge—maybe the best views anywhere, if you also want to see the other two members of Alaska's most famous mountain family: 17,400-foot Sultana and 14,570-foot Begguya. Officially named Mount Foraker in 1899—after Ohio Senator Joseph Benson Foraker, who eventually retired from politics in disgrace—the Alaska Range's second-highest peak also has two Tanaina Indian names. The better-known one is Sultana, "The Woman"; the other is Menlale, or "Denali's Wife." Seen from Anchorage, Sultana and Denali appear as twin mountain giants, nearly identical in height; but from the Peters Hills, it's clear that the shorter Sultana sits to the left of her imposing spouse. Between the couple is the range's third-highest peak. Like the other two, it stands grandly

MOSQUITOES AND OTHER PESKY CRITTERS

Alaska is home to at least 28 known species of mosquitoes. The most common varieties belong either to the *Aedes* or *Culiseta* genus. *Culiseta* types are more commonly known as "snow mosquitoes." They're the large, slow-moving, and easy-to-smash kind that appear in early spring. *Aedes* are the smaller, fast-moving mosquitoes that drive Alaskan mammals—including *Homo sapiens*—crazy throughout most of the summer.

Alaska's mosquitoes usually begin appearing in April, right after the thaw, and remain active through September. Peak periods vary in different parts of the state; in Southcentral, numbers start to taper off by mid-July, while in the Arctic, mosquitoes are only then hitting their stride. In most areas of the state, June to July is considered the peak mosquito period. They inhabit virtually all landscapes, from coastal forests to alpine tundra, but are especially thick in wet areas.

As Alaska mosquito expert Bill Burgoyne points out, "Flies bite; mosquitoes pierce and suck." Although mosquitoes use carbon dioxide, heat, and moisture to identify their victims, often the first thing that grabs their attention is silhouetted body form. They tend to be attracted to dark-colored clothing—black, navy blue, brown, or red. Perhaps it absorbs sunlight and acts as a heat producer.

Once they've found a victim, mosquitoes puncture the skin, then insert two tubes, one containing mosquito saliva, the other used for blood removal. The saliva includes an anticoagulant that prevents the blood from clotting during an attack. It's that anticoagulant that produces the welts and itching with which we're all too familiar. Baking soda is one remedy for mosquito-induced itches; solutions with camphor have also proved effective.

Humans aren't primary mosquito targets in Alaska, but we have to suffice when bears, moose, sheep, deer, wolves, caribou, and various smaller mammals aren't available. A number of weapons have been created to help humans deal with attacks. Number 1 is DEET (otherwise known as N,N-diethyl-toluamide). Developed during World War II, this chemical somehow confuses mosquitoes' sensory systems and tricks them into thinking there's no flesh nearby that's worth drilling. Because of its effectiveness, DEET is the active ingredient in nearly all commercial insect repellents. Some notable exceptions include Avon's perfumed bath oil Skin-So-Soft (believe it or not). There are also natural repellents that have been used for generations, including raw or cooked garlic and pennyroyal, citronella, and other herbs.

Other insect pests include biting flies and gnats. In Alaska, two in particular can be troubling: no-see-ums are tiny, gray, silver-winged gnats whose prick-like bites produce small red spots and, of course, an itch; white sox, small black flies with white legs, often take a small chunk of flesh when biting and leave a large, inflamed (and itchy) swelling that may remain for several days. Even more than mosquitoes, both white sox and no-see-ums have a talent for finding their way under loose clothing or into hair or ears. They too react to repellents, but seem less deterred than mosquitoes.

above the mountain crowd. It would follow then, that this third giant is "Denali's Child." Or so Alaska's Interior Natives believed, calling the mountain Begguya. English-speaking mapmakers decided otherwise and named it Mount Hunter, after an Easterner—Anna Falconett Hunter—who never saw the peak.

My first morning in the hills, the Alaska Range is shrouded in clouds, so instead of Denali gazing, I take a leisurely walk up to Long Point. It's only the beginning of September, but already alpine bearberry leaves flow crimson across the slopes, blueberry leaves are purplish red, willow leaves are yellow. But not all of the tundra's summer verdancy has been lost; grasses have yet to turn, and the shiny leaves of the evergreen mountain cranberry won't change at all.

In contrast with these autumnal reds and golds, temperatures are positively summer-like—the weekend's high will approach 60°F—and swarms of insects fill the air. Most aren't interested in human flesh or blood, but there are enough mosquitoes and biting flies to be an annoyance. White sox, small black flies with white-tipped legs, swarm when the wind dies down, so I hope for steady breezes. Another, more-pleasant summer remnant is the wildflowers. Most have already gone to seed, but a few hardy late bloomers are scattered among the berries: ground-hugging mountain harebells, their sky blue petals perched on inch-high stems; pink mats of moss campion; and, in protected creek swales, fuchsia fireweed spikes.

Even before reaching 3,929-foot Long Point, I can imagine why painter Sydney Laurence might have come here. The higher I climb, the more the world opens up in every direction. When there's nowhere higher to go, I pick out familiar landmarks. To the east and northeast are the glacially muddied Chulitna River, the dirty snout of the Ruth Glacier, and several places I've visited this summer: the Parks Highway, Byers Lake, Kesugi Ridge. Due south are vast lowlands

► A wilderness traveler looks toward Denali from the Peters Hills.

that stretch to Cook Inlet, 100 miles away, while to the southwest are the Yenlo Hills and, beyond them, Mount Susitna, a gentle hill I'm more used to seeing from Anchorage as the legendary "Sleeping Lady." Immediately to the southwest and west are the Peters Hills and Dutch Hills, then several waves of unnamed hills and valleys, and, finally, the Alaska Range.

Following the range's sweep from west to north, I come full circle to the glaciers, valleys, and mountains that form Denali's frontispiece. With its heights hidden by clouds, the northern landscape's most eye-catching element is the Tokositna Glacier. Fed by dozens of pale blue fingers, it cuts through steep-sided peaks, then snakes between dark green forested foothills. The glacier, in turn, feeds the Tokositna River, a braided, silt-laden stream that bends around the base of the Peters Hills. Born in the national park, much of the Tokositna River meanders through Little Denali, and it is one of the state park's few floatable waterways.

Shortly after noon, the thick overcast begins to rupture and Denali's upper reaches poke above the clouds. This partial unveiling starts me thinking about Sydney Laurence. Widely regarded as Alaska's preeminent landscape artist, Laurence is best known for his early 20th-century paintings of what art historian Kesler Woodward calls "a romantic and unspoiled Alaska." Born in Brooklyn in 1868, he learned to paint in New York and Europe, then abandoned a promising career in 1904 to prospect for Alaskan gold.

Once in Alaska, Laurence hardly touched a paintbrush or canvas until 1912. A year later, given a grubstake and outfitted with a sled dog team, he headed north in the dead of winter to paint Denali's portrait. The 400-mile trip took March, April, and May to complete (the journey made more difficult by the fact that Laurence was still on crutches from a shipwreck accident). Once there, he was forced to return to Seward to pick up art supplies, on order from Seattle, before starting work. By fall, Laurence had completed 43 studies of the mountain. The final painting, a 6-by-12-foot oil on canvas titled *Mount McKinley* and now owned by the

Anchorage Museum of History and Art, is regarded as one of his crowning achievements.

There would be other trips, other McKinley paintings. Whether they were inspired by the view at Long Point is debatable. None of the perspectives, or the description of his camp, seems to fit. No matter. Whether he stood here or 5 miles away, Laurence's spirit and connection to Denali touch these hills.

The Peters Hills, like Kesugi Ridge, are not much to look at from a distance. Fifteen miles long and four miles wide, these gently rounded, tundra-topped knobs and ridgelines barely reach 4,000 feet. Both they and the nearby Dutch Hills are dissected by dozens of small clear-water streams. That, in itself, is not unusual. What's special about these creeks is that so many are named. There's Coal, Slate, Divide, Bunco, and Poorman Creeks, and Lunch, Fox, Davies, and Pioneer Gulches. Look closely enough at maps of the area and you'll also find symbols for buildings, landing strips, and mines. There's even a road—and a mostly deserted nearby community—named Petersville. Nearly all the construction, and the naming, was done in the early 1900s by gold miners. Once ranked among Alaska's major placer gold districts, the Petersville region now yields little ore. Instead of gold, recreation brings people to the area: hiking and backpacking in summer, hunting in fall, snowmobiling in winter. And, of course, there's the view of Denali.

Only the northeastern corner of the Peters Hills, maybe 10 square miles, lies within Denali State Park. It was added in 1976, part of a 42,000-acre expansion. And once again, tourism played a role. The Peters Hills, many bureaucrats and politicians felt, would be the perfect place to put a visitor center. By making a portion of the hills parkland, the state could protect the area from conflicting development.

The first person to target the Peters Hills was neither an Alaskan nor a politician, but a visionary New Englander whose name is intimately tied to Denali: Bradford Washburn. A highly successful mountaineer, photographer, author, cartographer, and scientist,

▲ Autumn in Denali: Yellow-leafed birches and dark green spruce are reflected in Byers Lake, easily accessible from the Parks Highway.

Washburn is widely considered the world's leading authority on Mount McKinley; since the mid-1930s, he's devoted much of his life to its study and exploration. In the early 1950s, and again in the late 1960s and mid-1970s, Washburn proposed Long Point as the site of a simply built visitor center and lodge that would "not be an intrusion into the wilderness . . . [but] would give large numbers of people an opportunity to see real wilderness."

But simplicity wasn't what Alaska Senator Mike Gravel had in mind when he visited the Peters Hills in the late 1970s. Standing at Long Point, Gravel envi-sioned "Denali City," a huge Teflon-domed structure just above the Tokositna River. Within the climate-controlled dome would be hotels, shopping centers, condominiums, and golf courses, plus a cultural and international trade center. Next to the city, there'd be a downhill ski resort. And an aerial tramway would take passengers across the Tokositna to a restaurant and observation deck in the Tokosha Mountains.

As strange as it sounds now, Gravel's proposal was taken seriously in some political quarters. Reflecting the anything-is-possible attitudes inspired by Prudhoe Bay and the Trans-Alaska Pipeline, the state senate in

93

1980 appropriated $1 million for an in-depth look at Gravel's "recreational community," minus the dome. Washburn wasn't nearly as thrilled: "McKinley needs something more," he told a reporter. "But the things Mike is talking about are not the things that I am. . . . I just hope I haven't lighted a campfire that is going to burn down the forest." Washburn needn't have worried. Neither his, nor Gravel's, vision has so far led to any development in the Peters Hills.

Still, the idea of a South Denali visitor complex simply won't die. On the same day that I hike into the Peters Hills—15 years after Mike Gravel proposed his grand vision—the *Anchorage Daily News* publishes a story headlined "NEW ANGLE ON DENALI PROPOSED." The gist of the story: a task force studying Denali National Park issues has recommended that a "modest" visitor center with hiking trails, campground, and public-use cabins be built in the Tokositna River valley below the Peters Hills. For it to work, the Petersville Road would have to be upgraded and extended several miles.

Pat Pourchot, a former state senator and task force member, says the Tokositna facility will boost tourism and give Alaskans easier access to Denali National Park. The funny thing is, though, that the group's preferred site is within Denali *State* Park, less than 3 miles from Long Point. Another task force member emphasizes: "We are talking about the area where Sydney Laurence painted his paintings. It's such an incredible place."

I agree. It's incredible. Not only the scenery, but the wildness, the solitude, the primeval essence of the place. Except for some abandoned weather-station clutter at Long Point and occasional rock cairns, this northern end of the Peters Hills remains free of human signs. And few people travel the 4 to 5 miles—much of it uphill, across untrailed tundra and through dense willow thickets—that it takes to reach the state park. In 3 days, I see only two other people here.

By some strange twist of circumstances, I've brought the September 1, 1994, edition of the *Daily News* with me into the Peters Hills, and open it to the South Denali story as I'm sitting down to dinner. I'm shocked, angered, storming to myself, *No. Not here. Go build your tourist mecca somewhere else. Why should the wildness of Denali State Park be sacrificed to solve the national park's visitor dilemmas?*

Oddly enough, signs of human presence already exist in the valley below. A primitive road and, beyond that, an ATV trail wind along the base of the neighboring Dutch Hills. With binoculars I can see some shacks and a pickup. And 4 miles west of camp is a placer gold operation with several trailers, machinery, and mine tailings. Somehow none of that bothers me as much as the proposed visitor center. The miners were here long before the park; they built Petersville Road and opened this land to hunters and hikers and backpackers. There's been no large or hideous scarring of the landscape, and the miners aren't encroaching on protected parkland. Besides, they tell stories of the region's past, not its future. Large-scale "industrial" tourism, not mining, is the looming shadow here.

Sunday morning, my last in the Peters Hills, brings subfreezing temperatures: water left in a pot overnight is glazed with ice, and both tent and tundra are heavily frosted. It also brings clear skies and the Alaska Range panorama I've been hoping to see. The mountains are still in predawn shadow when I emerge from the tent at 6:30. I get the stove going to boil water for coffee, then grab camera gear and a granola bar, and rush back to find a place among the lichen-covered rocks above camp. There's no need to walk to Long Point for this morning's show.

Day's first light touches Denali shortly before 7. It suffuses the mountaintop with a pale pink glow, then gently washes across the range, giving definition and depth to what had been a flat gray silhouette. It's a familiar view, not far different from the one we have in Anchorage. But here in the Peters Hills, I have a front-row seat, one that offers infinitely more detail. The monolithic wall of mountains seen from town now becomes a granitic sea of serrated ridges, spiked towers, and immense rock faces. And behind the first dark waves of mountains stand the three ice giants, looming

TRUMPETER SWANS

▲ Trumpeter swans cross Byers Lake in early September. This pair returns each summer to breed.

Trumpeter swans once inhabited much of North America, but the birds were hunted almost to extinction by the early 1900s. In 1932, biologists could account for only 69 trumpeters, but it's likely that many more went uncounted in Alaska, where they were first identified in 1850 but not confirmed as breeders until 1954.

In 1968—the year that trumpeters were removed from the endangered species list—federal biologists counted more than 2,800 of the swans state-wide. And in 1990, researchers found more than 13,000 trumpeters in Alaska, about 80 percent of the world's population.

Among the species that choose mates for life, trumpeters raise broods of two to seven young, called cygnets. When they fledge after 11 to 15 weeks, they're close to adult size: females average 22 pounds, males 28, though some weigh up to 40 pounds. The largest member of the waterfowl family and one of three swans to seasonally reside in Alaska—the others are the tundra swan and the Asian whooper swan—the trumpeter is found in forested wetlands, lakes, marshes, and rivers from the Panhandle to the Yukon River. It's a seasonal resident of several Alaska state parks, including Denali, Chugach, Wood-Tikchik, and Kachemak Bay.

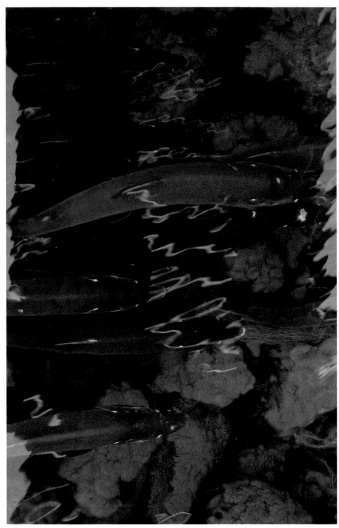

▲ Sockeye salmon enter Byers Lake, where they'll spawn and die.

better place to see Denali and its family. And I wonder: can Denali possibly cast such a spell on someone who's watching from a hectic, crowded visitor center? Perhaps there's a way to make the South Denali project work, without losing the wild essence of these hills. I can't imagine how.

⚊〰⚊

MID-SEPTEMBER, Byers Lake. A cold drizzle falls as I walk to the lakeshore campground, 2 miles from the road. Sockeye have again returned to spawn and die, and many decomposing bodies already float lifelessly along the shore or lie along the lake bottom. Others, just now arriving, have crimson bodies and olive green heads. Near the campground, two trumpeter swans swim serenely offshore, occasionally dunking their heads to feed on lake-bottom plants. Summer residents of Byers Lake, they'll soon depart for coastal wintering grounds. Later, more than 30 mergansers dabble in shallow waters nearby. Fish-eating diving ducks, they too are local summer residents who'll soon fly south. As though in training for their flight, several adolescent mergansers vigorously flap their wings.

The campground is deserted, and I have the pick of six sites. I pitch my tent, then go down to the lake. Three dozen sockeye swim offshore and several male-female pairs guard nest sites, where muck and other debris have been cleared away to reveal a white, sandy lake bottom. The salmon circle relentlessly, in a sort of mating dance, and aggressively attack any fish that intrude upon their space. Soon eggs will be laid and fertilized and the salmon will die, adding nutrients to the lake system. A final gift to their offspring.

By 7:30 P.M. the drizzle has become a steady downpour. There'll be no one else staying here tonight. And no views of Denali. Within a week or two the rain will be replaced by snow, and soon after that the campgrounds will close for winter. Lulled to sleep by tapping rain, I spend my last night in Denali State Park dreaming of swans and great ice mountains. In the morning, I too will be headed south for winter.

above the rest. The color and intensity of light rapidly change, with rose turning to yellow, then eventually to white under the sun's glare. I scan Denali's ridges and walls with binoculars; they look so forbidding, unassailable. It seems a lifetime ago that I stood upon that mountain.

Touched by a presence that's inspired painters, poets, and climbers, I realize it's true: there may be no

▲ **Ptarmigan**

IF YOU GO

Getting There: Adjacent to the southeastern corner of Denali National Park and Preserve, 325,460-acre "Little Denali" is one of Alaska's most accessible parklands. It's bisected by the George Parks Highway, the major road link between Anchorage and Fairbanks, which crosses Denali's southern boundary at MP 132, about a 2½-hour drive north of Anchorage, then passes through the park for 37 miles. The park's western fringes can be reached via Petersville Road, which intersects the Parks Highway at MP 115; high-clearance, four-wheel-drive vehicles are recommended beyond mile 18. Once inside the park, most visitors keep to the road corridor. Backcountry travel is mostly by foot or boat in summer, or by ski, dogsled, or snowmobile in winter.

Weather: Denali State Park is in a transition zone between the moist and cool maritime climate to the south and the drier, warmer interior climate to the north. Overcast skies are the summer norm, with daytime temperatures ranging from the 40s into the 70s. Winter temperatures may range from 30°F to -40°F.

When to Go: Visitors can drive through Denali State Park year-round, but most public facilities are closed from October through April. The prime time for hiking and backpacking is June through September; snow machining, mushing, and skiing are popular in winter.

Facilities and Services: Denali has three road-accessible campgrounds: Lower Troublesome Creek, Byers Lake, and Denali View North. Byers Lake also has a hike-in/boat-in "lakeshore" campground. Two public-use cabins at Byers Lake are available year-round. Equipped with bunks, woodstove, table, and benches, they must be reserved in advance; check with the Division of Parks for costs. Other park facilities include "Denali View" turnouts and interpretive sites at MPs 135.2 and 162.4, and the Kesugi Ridge trail network. Several guides and outfitters offer trips into Denali State Park. Information on those businesses, and nearby lodges, can be obtained from the area superintendent's office (see below).

Activities: The park is perhaps best known for its views of 20,320-foot Mount McKinley, and Denali-viewing is by far the most popular activity. Other recreational uses include camping, hiking, backpacking, berry picking, river floating, wildlife watching, fishing, hunting, skiing, mushing, and snowmobiling.

Hiking: Trailheads are located at Upper Troublesome Creek (MP 137.6), Byers Lake (MP 147), Ermine Hill (MP 156.5), and Little Coal Creek (MP 163.9). The main Kesugi Ridge–Troublesome Creek Trail is 36 miles long and has an elevation gain of about 3,500 feet; above treeline the trail is marked by rock cairns, but map-reading and route-finding skills are recommended. Within the trail system are several shorter routes, rated easy to difficult. The Troublesome Creek Trailhead is usually closed from mid-July through September 1, because of possible human-bear conflicts. The Peters Hills in western Denali State Park offer excellent backpacking opportunities across trailless tundra.

For More Information: Contact the Mat-Su-Valdez-Copper River Area Superintendent, c/o Alaska State Parks, HC 32 Box 6706, Wasilla, AK 99654-9719; (907) 745-3975.

CHILKAT 6

ALASKA CHILKAT BALD EAGLE PRESERVE

A GATHERING OF EAGLES

The first bald eagle is spotted at Milepost 16 of the Haines Highway. White head and tail show it to be an adult, at least 5 years old. (Lacking the species' characteristic plumage, immature birds have a darker, mottled look.) The eagle isn't doing anything spectacular. It's not soaring, or diving, or feeding. It's simply sitting in a cottonwood, motionless except for its head, which it swivels our way as the bus slows.

Inside, a shout of "there's one, on the left" has stirred a flurry of activity. Some passengers grab for binoculars or cameras, while others put faces to windows. It's an unusual thing to be among nine Alaskans all intently focused on this one bird. Each of us has seen bald eagles before, many times. This is nothing new or especially exciting. But it's not the eagle that's got us stirred up. It's what the bird portends.

We pull over and spend a few moments of this early December morning in the company of the eagle, our greeter to one of the world's great wildlife feasts. Then, anxious to attend the banquet, we continue up the road, toward the heart of 48,000-acre Alaska Chilkat Bald Eagle Preserve. Within 5 minutes, we're surrounded by bald eagles. Dozens of them roost, like feathered holiday ornaments, in the large cottonwoods that line the highway. In one tree I count 12 eagles. Others sit immobile on the Chilkat River's snow-covered flats, circle and play in the sky, or pick at salmon carcasses.

◄ Bald eagles often sit in small groups when resting in the cottonwoods that line the Haines Highway, within the Chilkat preserve.
▲ An immature bald eagle roosts above the Chilkat River.

Two miles away, on the Chilkat River's opposite banks, are more cottonwoods and even larger concentrations of roosting eagles. Some trees have 30, 40 birds. In all, hundreds of bald eagles are visible, as well as smaller numbers of ravens, gulls, mergansers, and magpies. It's a sensory overload, for ears as well as eyes. In a talkative mood, the eagles chatter in a nonstop cacophony of high-pitched screeches and trills. They have curiously high voices for such large, predatory birds, not at all in keeping with their image.

Each autumn, for as long as anyone can remember, thousands of bald eagles have congregated in the Chilkat Valley, at the northern end of Alaska's Panhandle. Attracted by a late-fall run of chum salmon, they come from an area of more than 100,000 square miles. The majority reside in Southeast Alaska (200 to 400 are year-round residents), but tagging studies have shown that others, usually younger birds, travel here from British Columbia, the Yukon Territory, and Washington state.

This meeting of eagles, the largest in the world, is centered in a 5,000-acre Critical Habitat Area called the Bald Eagle Council Grounds. Here, for much of the winter, warm-water springs keep sections of the Chilkat River from freezing over, thus giving eagles easy access to a large supply of spawned-out chum salmon carcasses at a time of year when food is normally scarce. "Warm," of course, is a relative term. The spring waters that percolate into the Bald Eagle Council Grounds are, by most standards, quite chilly: 39°F to 43°F. They originate in an alluvial fan reservoir, a fan-shaped accumulation of boulders, gravel, sand, and glacial sediments at the Chilkat's confluence with two tributary rivers: the Tsirku and the Kleheni.

From spring through early fall, water accumulates in the Tsirku Fan to create a huge underground reservoir. When air temperatures drop in winter, the reservoir's subsurface waters are minimally affected; feeding the Chilkat from below, their warmer temperatures keep a 5-mile stretch of river open long after surrounding waters have frozen. Fortunately for the eagles, the upwelling groundwater aerates and cleans the river bottom to create exceptionally good salmon-spawning habitat. Lucky, too, that chums choose this open water to spawn, and that they enter the river through January; few of Alaska's salmon runs occur so late in the year. Sockeye and coho salmon also migrate up the Chilkat in winter, but they don't concentrate in the spring-fed portions of the stream and are, therefore, usually hidden from the eagles by ice.

Equally lucky are eagle watchers. The Bald Eagle Council Grounds are easily visible from the Haines Highway. And they're only a short drive from the town of Haines, which offers year-round visitor services. It's this unusual convergence of variables—winter, open water, chum salmon spawning grounds, eagles, highway, nearby comforts—that makes the Chilkat experience unique.

Large numbers of eagles normally arrive by October, with a population peak between mid-November and early December. Most leave by January, when salmon carcasses dwindle and the open river gradually freezes. Eagle numbers vary considerably from year to year, depending on the availability of food, which in turn depends primarily on weather and the strength of the salmon run. Since the late 1970s, when researchers began doing aerial surveys, annual peak counts have ranged from 1,000 to nearly 4,000 individuals. In 1984, the U.S. Fish and Wildlife Service recorded a "modern record" of 3,988 eagles; two years later, the count dropped to 1,124. More recently, from 1990 to 1994, annual highs ranged from 2,137 to 3,284 birds.

Two surveys are flown each year, weather permitting, but it's impossible to count every eagle. And some years, weather prohibits flying when their numbers are highest. Federal eagle specialist and Chilkat census taker Mike Jacobson admits, "In any given year, peak numbers can be missed." To supplement the fly-over censuses, state park ranger Bill Zack conducts weekly ground counts; less exact, they at least provide an index by which trends can be traced.

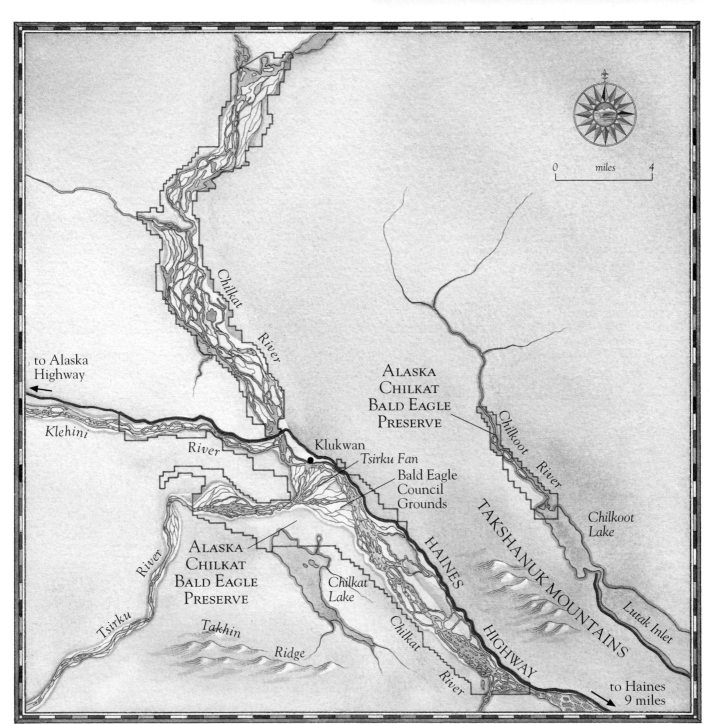

to Alaska
Highway

Klehini

River

ALASKA
CHILKAT
BALD EAGLE
PRESERVE

Klukwan

Tsirku Fan

Bald Eagle
Council
Grounds

Chilkoot River

CHILKAT

River

Chilkoot
Lake

Tsirku

River

ALASKA
CHILKAT
BALD EAGLE
PRESERVE

*Chilkat
Lake*

HAINES

TAKSHANUK MOUNTAINS

Lutak Inlet

Takhin

Ridge

Chilkat
River

HIGHWAY

to Haines
9 miles

0   miles   4

Some people claim that the Chilkat Valley once supported as many as 8,000 to 10,000 bald eagles. But after an intensive 4-year study (1979 to 1982), wildlife biologists Erv Boeker and Andy Hansen concluded that the Chilkat's eagle population "appears to be at the carrying capacity of its habitat. . . . It is likely that present population size and productivity are similar to presettlement levels." What that level is remains uncertain. Though he's counted as many as 3,700 eagles, Boeker believes "a lot more than that use the Chilkat. Birds move in and out."

Once the tour bus is parked in a designated turnout, we're turned loose into overcast, calm, 20°F weather. The ground rules are simple: stay out of traffic and off the flats (where the eagles feed), keep tripods off the pavement, and don't do anything to harass the birds. No trails or viewing decks have been built, so visitors must watch, photograph, and videotape the eagles from either the turnouts or the narrow wooded corridor between road and river channel.

Armed with camera gear, spotting scopes, and binoculars, we quickly disperse, as though some distance from each other will enhance our closeness to these great raptors. North America's second-largest birds of prey—only the California condor is bigger—adult bald eagles generally weigh 9 to 14 pounds (females of the species are largest) and have wing spans of 7½ feet. Though they often seem to glide slowly through the air, eagles can fly up to 30 miles per hour and may reach speeds of 100 miles per hour when diving.

As I walk to a neighboring turnout, it becomes clear that Chilkat's eagles have adapted well to motor-vehicle traffic. They pay little or no attention to the mechanized roar of cars and trucks that rumble past. Human traffic is not so universally tolerated. My presence unnerves, or perhaps merely annoys, a few of the eagles, who leave their cottonwood perches with slow-motion waves of their wings. Most, however, are content to nod their heads or stare impassively as I walk past.

Several roosting eagles sit with their wings extended downward. This "relaxation posture" helps them dry out feathers that get wet when they fish for salmon bodies. In winter's cold, bald eagles feed almost exclusively on dead or dying salmon. Capturing an active fish requires a high-energy expenditure that they can't afford. The choicest foods are fish carcasses that have been partially eaten—which eliminates the need to tear through tough skin—or recently submerged. Fish exposed to the air soon freeze and become inedible.

An opening in the trees allows me a good view of the flats. Less than 10 yards away, chum salmon swim in one of the Chilkat River's open channels. Many have already spawned; their bodies decaying, they slowly fan their tail fins while awaiting death. Along the river bottom are the carcasses of two already dead. A third carcass, pulled up on the riverbank, is surrounded by three eagles. Only one eats; the others watch and wait their turn. Also watching in nearby cottonwoods are a dozen more eagles.

The feeding bird tears off a chunk of flesh, swallows it, then quickly looks around, making certain that no competitors are trying to cut in. Three times spectator eagles leave their roosts and swoop low over the gravel bar. The feeding eagle ducks its head, but keeps its grip on the salmon, and the challengers fly off. Finally, a rival comes in with wings and talons extended. Both the feeder and the two nearby observers screech loudly, but they jump clear and yield to the newcomer. They've been displaced, a biologist would say.

Though it looks combative, displacement behavior is, in some respects, a cooperative thing. Studies have shown that injuries rarely occur during such confrontations because eagles "attack" those rivals most likely to yield a carcass without a fight: smaller or less ravenous birds. And through their body language, food holders apparently show whether or not they'll aggressively defend their meal. Displacement, or pirating, can therefore be a highly efficient way of procuring a meal, often preferable to hunting.

Over the next 45 minutes, the ritual is repeated four more times. An eagle feeds for several minutes, then is chased from the carcass by a hungrier bird. Within an hour, all edible parts have been consumed and five eagles have shared in the meal. Whether they have all been adequately fed is hard to say; in their studies of Chilkat's eagles, Boeker and Hansen found that "food holders typically are displaced before feeding to satiation."

What neither they nor anyone else have yet determined are the food requirements of Chilkat eagles. But studies done elsewhere have shown that at subfreezing temperatures, eagles consume 10 percent or more of their body weight daily. For a 14-pound eagle, that's 1½ pounds of chum per day.

Despite all the prey that's available, there's remarkably little feeding out on the flats. Most of the eagles sit motionless, as though patiently awaiting their turn in the buffet line. This, too, is typical cold-weather behavior. Washington researchers found that eagles along the Nooksack River spend more than 90 percent of their time perching, 4 percent eating, and 3 percent flying. The reason is simple: to conserve energy.

At night, or even in daytime when the weather is harsh, Chilkat's eagles abandon the river flats and roost in cottonwoods or nearby old-growth spruce–hemlock forest. And on rare occasions, extended cold spells will drive them from the valley entirely. In November 1986, subzero temperatures caused most of the Bald Eagle Council Ground's river channels to freeze. Already stressed by wind, extreme cold, and a small chum run, the eagles had their salmon supply almost entirely cut off. The obvious solution: look elsewhere for food. In October, 1,124 eagles had been counted; on November 20, when numbers should have been at, or near, their peak, only 510 were seen. Exactly where the eagles went is unknown, but biologists agree they probably scattered to warmer saltwater areas where herring and other winter foods could be found.

Energy conservation isn't quite as critical when the weather is mild and food abundant. In September and October, and sometimes even into November, Chilkat's eagles are more likely to be spotted soaring or engaged

in a form of air play called "talon locking." Flying in pairs, the birds face each other and lock talons; one bird on top of the other, they tumble downward in a free fall.

—◆—

CHILKAT'S EAGLES ARE now considered a local, state, and national treasure. But less than four decades ago they were hunted as vermin, because of the widespread, and mistaken, belief that their appetite for salmon and small game posed a threat to commercial fishermen and trappers. From 1917 to 1952, more than 128,000 of Alaska's bald eagles were killed for territorial bounties of $1 to $2; many were taken in Chilkat Valley. The bounty on eagles ended in 1953; 6 years later, Alaska gained statehood status and its eagles gained federal protection through the National Bald Eagle Act of 1960. Still, some killing continued.

The Chilkat gathering, though recognized as unique, didn't receive any special protections until 1972, when the 5,000-acre Critical Habitat Area was established. Any activities that might threaten the eagles were prohibited within the new sanctuary, but surrounding eagle habitat remained open to resource development. For much of the next decade, conservationists and developers fought over the need for additional safeguards. In 1977, then-governor Jay Hammond proposed a state park within the Chilkat Valley, but local opposition killed the plan. Two years later, the state signed a long-term timber-sale contract with a Haines lumber company, allowing more than 10 million board feet to be harvested annually. The trees to be clear-cut were mostly in the Chilkat Valley, thereby threatening the river, its salmon, and its eagles.

What had been a largely local issue soon gained nationwide attention. In response to a growing public outcry—and one United States senator's proposal to establish a national wildlife refuge—Hammond in 1980 declared a moratorium on logging in the Chilkat Valley. He also directed $250,000 in state funding to the Chilkat bald eagle study already started

by Boeker and Hansen (and cosponsored by the National Audubon Society and the U.S. Fish and Wildlife Service).

Additional protection for the Chilkat eagles was finally secured when an advisory committee crafted a compromise acceptable to all parties. And in June 1982—200 years after the bald eagle had been chosen as America's emblem—Governor Hammond signed legislation that established the Alaska Chilkat Bald Eagle Preserve. Managed by the Division of State Parks with the help of a 12-member advisory council, the preserve is off-limits to mining and logging but open to such traditional uses as fishing, hunting, berry picking, and trapping. Chilkat is therefore unique among Alaska's state park units, in that its primary mission is to preserve wildlife and wildlife habitat.

Dave Cline, the National Audubon Society's Alaska representative and one who played a crucial role in the preserve's creation, later commented: "I know of no other resource controversy in Alaska where loggers, miners, commercial fishermen, conservationists, and borough, city, federal, and state officials all signed a page-and-a-half agreement that settled the issue."

Once deeply divided over the need to protect Chilkat's eagles, the community of Haines now overwhelmingly supports the preserve for a simple reason: economics. Over the past 15 years, with traditional resource industries such as mining and logging in decline, Haines has become increasingly dependent on tourism. And Chilkat's eagles are a big draw.

A half-hour drive from the Bald Eagle Council Grounds, this coastal town of about 1,200 people has become the gateway to the Chilkat preserve. Visitors can get here by ferry, plane, or car. About 12,000 people visit the preserve annually, mostly in summer. And nearly all spend time, and money, in Haines. Not surprisingly, businesses have begun to emphasize their community's eagle connection. "The preserve was created for the

105

◄ A bald eagle takes off with a salmon head, while a gull and a magpie look on.

eagles, not tourism. It just so happens to be along the highway—but that fact makes it a tourist attraction," says Ray Menaker, a longtime Haines resident who served on the preserve's advisory council for a decade. "A lot of people who didn't like the idea originally have become gung-ho, because of the added tourism in winter and late fall. The preserve has been a fortuitous thing. It's put Haines on the map. This is where the eagles are."

Haines and the mountains, lakes, rivers, and ocean that surround it have plenty to offer the summer tourist: salmon derbies, river trips, wildlife viewing, Native dancing, play productions, arts and crafts shows, camping, hiking, and a late-summer state fair. But there's little reason, besides Chilkat's eagles, to visit during the off-season. Though still comparatively small, winter use of the Chilkat preserve has grown sharply over the past decade, thanks largely to documentaries, magazine articles, and even a live broadcast, televised via satellite to a worldwide audience in 1986.

"That show was seen by millions of people," Menaker says. "Afterward, people called in from all over the place."

During the preserve's "high-exposure time" in the 1980s, ranger Bill Zack once counted 300 people watching eagles. But that's proved to be the exception. More typical are daily winter counts of 20 to 30 people, most of them amateur and professional photographers who stay in Haines for periods of a few days to a few weeks.

Twenty-one highway miles from Haines, cradled between the road and the Chilkat River, is a community with even closer connections to Chilkat's eagles: the Tlingit Indian village of Klukwan.

Klukwan's people have coexisted with eagles for centuries. Their small community (population about 100) sits adjacent to the council grounds, which they first named, and many of their rituals and artworks are tied to the eagles' presence. Yet they have mixed feelings about the preserve. Village leaders have occasionally talked of building an eagle-viewing center

and museum, but so far there's been no development. Residents remain leery of tourism, fearing they, as well as the eagles, will be put on view.

—◈—

SINCE ITS BIRTH in 1982, the Chilkat Bald Eagle Preserve has faced a long series of management challenges. Most have been small; others have seemed like impending crises. None, so far, has been insurmountable. One of the earliest issues involved visitor restrictions. Until the mid-1980s, most eagle watchers were content to stay in the narrow roadside corridor. But in 1986, low river levels made it easier to reach the council grounds. And competition among photographers for the "definitive" eagle picture prompted many to walk onto the flats and approach feeding birds. Some photographers went so far as to "bait" the eagles with salmon purchased at a local butcher shop.

In response, the Division of State Parks began a public-education program. Signs were posted within the preserve asking visitors to stay off the flats and refrain from disturbing eagles in any way, and a word-of-mouth campaign was also started. The education effort proved a huge, and almost immediate, success. "I think most of the photographers and sightseers appreciate the preserve for what it is," says Zack. "They don't want to intentionally harass the birds."

Another "people" issue, complicated by the lack of viewing stands and trails, has been public safety. The large numbers of eagles in cottonwoods along the highway prompt passing cars to stop, often without using turnouts or even pulling over. And photographers are easily tempted to set up their tripods on the pavement. By the end of the 1980s, the Division of State Parks had established a set of visitor guidelines to protect both eagles and humans. Chief among them are requests that visitors stay off the flats, view eagles in an area between the highway and river, not disturb the salmon, and park only in designated turnouts.

As the preserve approached its 10th anniversary in 1992, visitor conduct had become less troubling than salmon behavior. Three straight years of abnormally low chum returns prompted fears of a salmon crash—and a subsequent end to the world's largest bald eagle gathering. "The only way to properly manage for the eagles is to manage for the fish. Without the salmon, you're not going to have large numbers of eagles," warned Haines photographer Erich von Stauffenberg, then cochair of the preserve's advisory panel.

Also worried was Ray Staska, a commercial fisheries biologist in Haines: "We can only speculate about what's been happening with the salmon. It could be a problem with the food chain, it could be high-seas fishing, it could be stream-channel changes [that eliminated some spawning grounds]. A big question now is whether the number of chums will become so low the eagles don't return."

Zack took a more moderate view: "What I hear a lot is, 'The preserve is falling, the preserve is falling.' I don't buy it. Chum returns have been down, but I haven't seen a steady downward trend of eagles." Mike Jacobson also saw no cause for alarm. Even as the chum returns dropped from 1989 through 1991, eagle numbers grew from 1,228 to 3,233, the most since 1984.

So far, the optimists have proved more prophetic than the doomsayers. By November 1994, the Chilkat River's late-run chums showed signs of recovering. Still, Staska cautions, chum numbers remain considerably lower than the long-term average of 250,000 fish.

There have been other concerns: a proposed copper mine in neighboring British Columbia, land disputes, commercial river rafting, and the threat of clear-cut timber harvesting on state forest land adjacent to the preserve. The forest contains some of the region's better timber, but its trees also provide eagle nesting sites and they're heavily used for roosting during winter storms and extreme cold.

Beneath the resource and human issues is a more deep-rooted and, so far, insoluble problem: insufficient money to manage the preserve and study its resources properly. No comprehensive studies of the Chilkat's eagles have been done since 1982, and much still needs to be learned about eagle behavior and food and habitat requirements. More also should be known about the salmon, the river, the forest, the valley's other wildlife, and the ways they interconnect with each other and the eagles.

Insufficient funding isn't unique to the Alaska Chilkat Bald Eagle Preserve; it's a system-wide dilemma, a reflection of declining state revenues. Still, folks like Menaker and von Stauffenberg find it painfully ironic that the state has spent "millions" to promote the preserve but almost nothing to operate it. "The legislation that created the preserve says its primary purpose is to protect the bald eagles and their essential habitat in perpetuity," von Stauffenberg says. "To me that means forever. But how are we going to do that without funding? And when will the preserve get its much-delayed visitor facilities?"

Zack, as usual, offers a moderate view: "Progress has been slow, but we're making headway. Certainly we could use more visitor facilities, and I'd like to see more studies of the eagles and salmon. But you just have to roll with the punches and accept that things are slowly improving."

One major improvement is scheduled for 1996: using federal funds, the state is building an open-air shelter with interpretive displays and a brand-new pullout with room for up to 20 vehicles and six buses. There's even hope that a trail may finally be completed.

―⁓―

NOVEMBER 1994. I've returned to Chilkat Valley for the third time in 8 years, but my timing is lousy: the weather is the stormiest it's been all season. More than 2½ feet of snow fall during my 5-day stay, and when it's not snowing, high winds kick up a ground blizzard and drive windchill temperatures to -40°F. Wicked stuff for both eagles and eagle watchers.

Heavy, drifting snow keeps me in Haines for 2 days. Two others are only marginally better, but I dig out the rental car and head for the Bald Eagle Council Grounds. Winds and below-zero chill have driven the

▲ The Chilkat Valley's gathering of eagles is concentrated in the Bald Eagle Council Grounds. Hundreds of the birds can often be spotted on gravel bars or in trees.

eagles off the flats into the trees. A couple of hundred roost in cottonwoods along the highway, but most have fled to the relative comfort of old-growth Sitka spruce and hemlock in neighboring Haines State Forest. Nearly all the eagles sit immobile, hunched over, though a few hardy birds pick at partially frozen carcasses on the riverbank.

Yet for all the gloom and cold, there's one morning when I catch a break in the weather. Bill Zack is kind enough to give me a ride to the preserve through still-unplowed streets, and we find the valley rich with birds: mergansers, ravens, gulls, chickadees, magpies, Steller jays. And lots of eagles. More than I've ever seen. Zack tells me that 2,137 eagles were counted on the year's first survey flight. And the salmon return looks healthy. Two pieces of good news. We walk along the highway to a spot that offers a panoramic view of the council grounds. Then Zack hands me his binoculars and challenges me: "See how many you can count."

First I do the flats, where hundreds of eagles sit on stumps, snags, boulders, and snow-covered ground, and count 590. Next, the cottonwoods. Eyesight beginning to blur, I slowly scan the distant trees, trying to somehow keep track of the tiny, dark shapes. I estimate 360 more, 950 in all. We trade glances, then smiles. It's a place of wonder, this valley of the eagles.

▲ **Screeching eagle**

IF YOU GO

Getting There: The 48,000-acre Chilkat preserve is located near the coastal community of Haines, at the northern end of Alaska's Panhandle. Haines can be reached by air, ferry, or state highway. From there, it's only 10 miles by car to the preserve, and about 18 miles to the Bald Eagle Council Grounds. The Haines Highway cuts through the preserve and offers excellent eagle-viewing opportunities; the main gathering of eagles is easily visible from the roadside, between MPs 18 and 22.

Weather: From October through December, the main eagle-viewing period, visitors should expect cold, wet, and often stormy weather. Temperatures may rise above freezing or fall below zero. Strong winds often blow through the valley, occasionally dropping windchills to -40°F or below.

When to Go: Between 200 and 400 bald eagles live in the Chilkat Valley year-round, but eagles from other regions begin to gather in early fall. For prime eagle viewing, the Alaska Division of Parks recommends November, when numbers are usually at their peak. The first half of December generally offers excellent eagle watching as well, but the weather is more severe and extended cold spells sometimes prompt the birds to disperse.

Facilities and Services: After years with no public facilities, the preserve is scheduled to get an open-air shelter with interpretive displays and a large new pullout in 1996. There are tentative plans for a roadside trail. Campgrounds in nearby Chilkat State Park and two state recreation sites are closed during the prime eagle-viewing period. Haines offers a full range of visitor services, including car rentals and year-round guided tours into the preserve. The town is also the headquarters of the American Bald Eagle Foundation, with a visitor center and natural history exhibits. And in November 1995, Haines hosted its first-ever Alaska Bald Eagle Festival.

Activities: In winter, eagle watching and photography. In summer, wildlife viewing and photography, river floating, and fishing.

For More Information: Contact Alaska State Parks, 400 Willoughby Avenue, Third Floor, Juneau, AK 99801; (907) 465-4563). Or call the ranger office in Haines, at (907) 766-2292. For information on visitor services, contact the Haines Visitor Bureau, Box 530, Haines, AK 99827; (907) 766-2234. For details about the American Bald Eagle Foundation, call founding member Dave Olerud at (907) 766-2441. Another resource is the book *The Bald Eagle: Haunts and Habits of a Wilderness Monarch*, by Jon Gerrard and Gary Bortolotti.

▼ **Photographers brave a Chilkat Valley snowstorm.**

OTHER SPECIAL ALASKA STATE PARKS

Alaska's state parklands reach more than 1,100 miles across the state, from Dall Bay State Marine Park near Ketchikan to Wood-Tikchik State Park in the Bristol Bay region and Upper Chatanika River State Recreation Site, just north of Fairbanks. Nearly 130 in all, they include recreation sites and areas, historic sites and parks, marine parks, wilderness parks, state trails, and a preserve. The largest unit, Wood-Tikchik, encompasses 1.6 million acres, nearly half the system's entire area. The smallest—Wickersham State Historic Site in Juneau and the Potter Section House in Anchorage—are less than an acre.

The park units are grouped into six management areas: Southeast, Kodiak, Kenai Peninsula, Chugach–Southwest, Matanuska–Susitna–Valdez–Copper River Basin, and Northern. Facilities for each of the areas are summarized below. For this section, I've grouped these management areas under geographic zones, with area office information, summaries of facilities, and brief descriptions of five other "special places."

A pamphlet with locator map and listings for all the state park units is available from Alaska State Parks offices and from Alaska Public Lands Information Centers in Anchorage and Fairbanks.

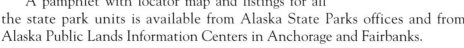

◀ Independence Mine State Historical Park is located in Southcentral Alaska's Talkeetna Mountains, near Hatcher Pass.
▲ Visitors can expect to encounter sea otters within the Prince William Sound Marine Parks.

SOUTHEAST ALASKA

SOUTHEAST MANAGEMENT AREA

Area Office: 400 Willoughby Avenue, Third Floor, Juneau, AK 99801; (907) 465-4563.

Summary of Facilities: The area's 32 units include 15 marine parks, ranging in size from 62 to 3,560 acres. Most are remote and undeveloped and accessible only by plane or boat. Of the Southeast units, four near Haines and one near Ketchikan have road-accessible campgrounds with toilet facilities and drinking water. Others feature trails, historic sites, or sportfishing. The area's prime attraction is the Alaska Chilkat Bald Eagle Preserve.

A Special Place: *Totem Bight State Historical Park,* near Ketchikan on Revillagigedo Island, is dedicated to Southeast Alaska's Native peoples and cultures. This road-accessible 11-acre unit has an interpretive trail that winds through coastal rain forest and connects 14 respresentative Tlingit and Haida totem poles and a clan house. The park also offers an excellent view of Tongass Narrows, one of the many saltwater channels that make up the Panhandle's "Inside Passage."

SOUTHCENTRAL AND SOUTHWESTERN ALASKA

KODIAK MANAGEMENT AREA

Area Office: Mile 3.5 Mill Bay Road, SR Box 3800, Kodiak, AK 99615; (907) 486-6339.

Summary of Facilities: The area's 5 units include 2 remote parks and 3 that can be reached by road from Kodiak. Fort Abercrombie and the Buskin River and Pasagshak State Recreation Sites each have campgrounds, with a total of 40 sites. All 3 campgrounds have toilets and running water; 2 have picnic shelters and trail systems.

A Special Place: *Fort Abercrombie State Historical Park,* perched on a forested headland at the northern end of Kodiak Island, can be reached by car from the town of Kodiak (population about 7,200). Here, visitors can explore the remains of an artillery fort built during World War II. Facilities include a campground, picnic area, and coastal trails that wind through meadows and Sitka spruce rain forest. A ranger station provides information about the site.

KENAI PENINSULA MANAGEMENT AREA

Area Office: Mile 85 Sterling Highway, P.O. Box 1247, Soldotna, AK 99669; (907) 262-5581.

Summary of Facilities: The 32 units include 19 undeveloped marine parks and numerous recreation areas and sites along the highway system, as well as Kachemak Bay State Park and Wilderness Park. Of the 32 units, 18 have campgrounds with toilets and running water, 7 have picnic shelters, 6 have boat launches, and nearly all offer fishing opportunities.

A Special Place: *The Prince William Sound State Marine Parks* include 14 different units, ranging from 370 to 4,560 acres. All are undeveloped and accessible only by boat or plane (most easily out of Seward, Whittier, or Cordova). Tucked into a corner of Alaska's Gulf Coast and separated from the rest of Southcentral Alaska by a wall of rugged mountains and massive ice fields, Prince William Sound is considered one of the state's premier coastal "playgrounds," with recreational opportunities for boaters, anglers, hunters, hikers, wildlife watchers, and beachcombers; it's especially popular with sea kayakers. Most of the parks are within 20 miles of either Whittier or Cordova.

CHUGACH–SOUTHWEST MANAGEMENT AREA

Area Office: HC52, P.O. Box 8999, Indian, AK 99540; (907) 345-5014.

Summary of Facilities: The 2 units in this area are Chugach and Wood-Tikchik State Parks.

MATANUSKA–SUSITNA–VALDEZ–COPPER RIVER BASIN MANAGEMENT AREA

Area office: HC32, P.O. Box 6706, Wasilla, AK 99687; (907) 745-3975 or (907) 822-5536 (in Glennallen).

Summary of Facilities: Stretching from Valdez north to Glennallen, then west to Willow and Denali State Park, this area includes 26 units, all of them accessible from the state's highway system. Among the facilities are 24 campgrounds (most with drinking water, all with toilets), 14 picnic sites, nearly 30 trails, and 11 boat launches. Most also feature sportfishing for salmon, trout, or grayling.

A Special Place: *Nancy Lake State Recreation Area,* known for both its canoe routes and public-use cabins, is located near the town of Willow (about 1½ hours, by car, north of Anchorage). This 22,685-acre unit encompasses more than 130 lakes and ponds, many of them connected by canoe-system trails. Popular year-round, the Nancy Lake SRA is used heavily in summer by boaters and anglers, and in winter by skiers, mushers, and snowmobilers. Its public-use cabins are a special attraction; four are within a short hike of the road system, while eight others are more remote and accessible by the canoe-trail system.

INTERIOR REGION

NORTHERN MANAGEMENT AREA

Area Office: 3700 Airport Way, Fairbanks, AK 99709-4613; (907) 451-2695.

Summary of Facilities: The area's 16 units are accessible from the road system in Alaska's Interior. Most are within a 2-hour drive of Fairbanks. Among the facilities are 19 campgrounds, 15 picnic areas (8 with shelters), 14 trails, and 10 boat launches.

A Special Place: *Chena River State Recreation Area,* less than 1 hour's drive east of Fairbanks, is one of Interior Alaska's principal year-round playgrounds. Straddling the river for which it's named, the 254,000-acre area encompasses forested lowlands, alpine ridges, and historic trails. Popular summertime activities include canoeing the Chena River, camping, fishing, wildlife watching, and hiking the alpine country; in winter, the area is heavily used by snow machiners, nordic skiers, and dog mushers. Wildlife is abundant and includes moose, black and grizzly bears, and, rarely, wolves and wolverines. Facilities include 2 road-accessible campgrounds (with a total of 61 sites), trails, and a picnic area. Boats can put into the Chena River at several road-accessible sites.

▼ A lucky angler with her king-sized salmon, at the Kenai River Special Management Area.

VIEWING AND PHOTOGRAPHING ALASKA'S WILDLIFE

▲ Telephoto lenses allow photographers to get close-up views while keeping their distance from wildlife, like these two dueling bull moose.

From the Chilkat Valley's gathering of eagles to the Chugach Mountains' Dall sheep, Alaska's state parks offer a wide variety of wildlife-viewing and photography opportunities. The following tips should help wildlife watchers:

■ Understand the animals you wish to watch or photograph. Learn their habits and where they're most likely to be found. Mammals and birds are often most active in the dawn and twilight hours. Some of Alaska's best wildlife viewing is in spring and late summer, during annual migrations.

■ Observe animals from a distance *they* consider safe. Approach slowly and quietly, avoiding sudden movements—or, even better, let the animal come to you. Don't sneak up on animals, and never chase them. Binoculars, spotting scopes, and telephoto lenses make it possible to get "close-up" views from a

◄ ▼ **Brown/grizzly bears and Dall sheep are among the many species of wildlife often seen within Alaska's state parks.**

distance. Professional wildlife photographers most commonly use telephoto lenses in the 300mm to 600mm range, but less-expensive 200mm lenses often are adequate. Many amateurs use zoom lenses (70mm to 210mm are popular), which offer versatility. Whenever you use large lenses, use some sort of support—a tripod or monopod, for example—in combination with a cable release, to minimize camera movement. Motor drives or auto-winders are helpful for capturing action sequences. Photographers shooting for publication must use slide film to ensure high-quality reproduction.

- Don't feed wildlife, and don't disturb nests.
- Never approach a large mammal, especially a moose or bear, that has young; the parent may charge to protect its offspring.
- Your chances of seeing wildlife diminish if you bring a dog into the backcountry, even if it's on a leash.
- Don't harass wildlife. Although it's not their intention, wildlife watchers and photographers occasionally harm wildlife by their actions. Harassment of animals is a growing concern among professional photographers and should be taken seriously by anyone interested in wildlife. You know you're harassing animals if you detect "any behavioral change that results from human presence." At the mild end of the harassment spectrum, animals may simply stop feeding or walk away; in more extreme cases, they may flee an area, abandon eggs and offspring, or charge. If an animal seems nervous or aggressive, chances are it's being harassed.

SUGGESTED READING

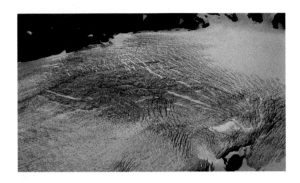

Alaska's Bears. Anchorage: Alaska Geographic Society, 1993.

The Alaska Wilderness Guide. Bellevue, Wash.: Vernon Publications, 1993.

Armstrong, Robert H. *Alaska's Birds: A Guide to Selected Species*. Seattle: Alaska Northwest Books, 1994.

——. *Guide to the Birds of Alaska*, 4th ed. Seattle: Alaska Northwest Books, 1995.

Caswell, Philip. *A Backcountry Naturalist's Guide to Wood-Tikchik State Park*. Anchorage: Nerka Press, in press.

Dowd, John. *Sea Kayaking: A Manual for Long-Distance Touring*. Seattle: University of Washington Press, 1988.

Ewing, Susan. *The Great Alaska Nature Factbook*. Seattle: Alaska Northwest Books, 1996.

Gerrard, Jon, and Gary Bortolotti. *The Bald Eagle: Haunts and Habits of a Wilderness Monarch*. Washington, D.C.: Smithsonian Institution Press, 1988.

Graydon, Don, ed. *Mountaineering: The Freedom of the Hills*, 5th ed. Seattle: Mountaineers, 1992.

Hansen, Andrew J., and others. *Bald Eagles of the Chilkat Valley, Alaska: Ecology, Behavior, and Management*. New York: National Audubon Society and U.S.F.W.S., 1984.

Herrero, Stephen. *Bear Attacks: Their Causes and Avoidance*. New York: Nick Lyons Books, 1985.

Jettmar, Karen. *The Alaska River Guide*. Seattle: Alaska Northwest Books, 1993.

Klein, Janet. *A History of Kachemak Bay, the Country, the Communities*. Homer: Homer Society of Natural History, 1987.

Nienhueser, Helen, and John Wolfe, Jr. *55 Ways to the Wilderness in Southcentral Alaska*. Seattle: Mountaineers, 1994.

O'Claire, Rita, Robert H. Armstrong, and Richard Carstensen. *The Nature of Southeast Alaska*. Seattle: Alaska Northwest Books, 1992.

Pratt, Verna. *Field Guide to Alaskan Wildflowers*. Anchorage: Alaskakrafts Publishing, 1989.

Savage, Candace. *Grizzly Bears*. San Francisco: Sierra Club, 1990.

Schofield, Janice. *Alaska's Wild Plants: A Guide to Alaska's Edible Harvest*. Seattle: Alaska Northwest Books, 1993.

——. *Discovering Wild Plants: Alaska, Western Canada, the Northwest*. Seattle: Alaska Northwest Books, 1989.

Sherwonit, Bill. *To the Top of Denali: Climbing Adventures on North America's Highest Peak*. Seattle: Alaska Northwest Books, 1990.

Smith, Dave, and Tom Walker. *Alaska's Mammals: A Guide to Selected Species*. Seattle: Alaska Northwest Books, 1995.

Walker, Tom. *Alaska's Wildlife*. Portland, Ore.: Graphic Arts Center Publishing, 1995.

Zimmerman, Jenny. *A Naturalist's Guide to Chugach State Park*. Anchorage, 1993.

◄ Park ranger Dave Johnston patrols Denali State Park in late winter. ▲ Glacier, Kachemak Bay State Park

INDEX

ABOUT THE AUTHOR

Outdoors/nature writer and photographer Bill Sherwonit has explored Alaska's state parks since the early 1980s. Born in Bridgeport, Connecticut, in 1950, Sherwonit earned an MS degree in geology from the University of Arizona. Switching careers in the late 1970s while in California, he returned to school and entered the field of journalism. In 1982 he joined the now-defunct *Anchorage Times*, working first as a sports writer, then as the newspaper's outdoors writer. Bill is now a full-time freelance writer and lives on Anchorage's Hillside, less than a mile from Chugach State Park. He writes for a wide variety of publications, including *ALASKA, Audubon, Climbing, National Parks, National Wildlife*, and *Summit* magazines. He has written two other books, *To the Top of Denali: Climbing Adventures on North America's Highest Peak* and *Iditarod: The Great Race to Nome*, and is contributing author for several guidebooks to Alaska. He teaches a nature writing class at the University of Alaska Anchorage.

ACKNOWLEDGMENTS

This book, for me, is in many ways a celebration of Alaska's state parks and the people responsible for their birth and continued well-being. Among the many people who've contributed to this project, I'm especially indebted to the park rangers and superintendents (past and present) who have shared their time, knowledge, and stories with me: Ed Apperson, Jill Holdren, Claire Holland, Dan Hourihan, Jeff Johnson, Dave Johnston, Roger MacCampbell, Al Meiners, Kevin Murphy, Pete Panarese, Dave Porter, and Bill Zack.

I'm grateful to all the park users and activists who have shared with me the stories of their relationships with Alaska's state parks, particularly Sharon Cissna, Art Davidson, Cliff Eames, Willie Hersman, Shawn Lyons, Mike and Diane McBride, Ray Menaker, *Jim Sayler, Erich von Stauffenberg, and Anne Wieland. Thanks also to all those who have supported Alaska's state parks over the years.*

Special thanks to Neil Johannsen, for writing the foreword and offering his recollections of Chugach State Park's early years; to my editors, Ellen Wheat and Nicky Leach, for their good advice, patience, and encouragement; to Betty Watson, for her wonderful design; to Laszlo Kubinyi, for his beautiful maps; to Kris Fulsaas, for her proofreading and organizational skills; to Sara Juday and Marlene Blessing, for backing the idea of this book; and to Dulcy Boehle, for her unwavering support.

Finally, I remain deeply grateful to the many people who've helped me along my writing path and provided ongoing inspiration.